1st EDITION

Perspectives on Diseases and Disorders

MRSA

Mary E. Williams

Book Editor

PERSPECTIVES
On Diseases & Disorders

GALE
CENGAGE Learning·

Detroit • New York • San Francisco • New Haven, Conn • Waterville, Maine • London

Elizabeth Des Chenes, *Director, Publishing Solutions*

For more information, contact:
Greenhaven Press
27500 Drake Rd.
Farmington Hills, MI 48331-3535
Or you can visit our Internet site at gale.cengage.com

For product information and technology assistance, contact us at

Gale Customer Support, 1-800-877-4253
For permission to use material from this text or product, submit all requests online at
www.cengage.com/permissions

Further permissions questions can be emailed to permissionrequest@cengage.com

LIBRARY OF CONGRESS CATALOGING-IN-PUBLICATION DATA

MRSA / Mary E. Williams, book editor.
   p. cm. -- (Perspectives on diseases and disorders)
 Includes bibliographical references and index.
 ISBN 978-0-7377-5779-8 (hardcover)
1. Staphylococcus aureus infections--Prevention. 2. Methicillin resistance. I. Williams, Mary E., 1960- II. Title: Methicillin-resistant staphylococcus aureus.
 QR201.S68M775 2012
 579.3'53--dc23
                          2012006807

Printed in the United States of America
2 3 4 5 6 7 16 15 14 13 12

CONTENTS

Brian Hoyle

Methicillin-resistant *Staphylococcus aureus*, or MRSA, is the bacterium that causes a potentially fatal staph infection that cannot be killed by commonly used antibiotics. Staph is normally present in the environment and usually remains harmless unless a drug-resistant form of it invades a wound or enters the body of a person with a compromised immune system.

Mary Quirk

The discovery of antibiotics in the middle of the twentieth century heralded an era of "miracle drugs" that prevented illness and death from bacterial diseases; however, widespread use of these drugs eventually led to the emergence of antibiotic-resistant "superbugs."

Denise Rinaldo

A growing number of teenagers across the United States are developing MRSA infections. Many of them are athletes, who are frequently in close contact with others. Equipment sharing and minor cuts and scrapes allow MRSA bacteria to enter the body and cause infection.

University of Chicago Medical Center

Two recent studies of staph infections in mice suggest that a vaccine for MRSA is possible. One potential vaccine could help destroy the bacteria's ability to evade the immune system, while another might counteract the germ's tissue-damaging mechanism.

CHAPTER 2   Controversies Concerning MRSA

Ian Lordon

The increase in MRSA infections over the past two decades corresponds with the transformation in meat production from small family farms to large factory farms. Cattle, pigs, and other livestock are given antibiotics as feed additives, resulting in the growth of antibiotic-resistant staph bacteria in the food supply and a higher rate of infectious illness.

Cliff Gauldin

MRSA has become more prevalent in pigs, and pork producers have a higher incidence of MRSA on their skin and in their nasal passages. Neither of these factors, however, bears any connection to an increase in MRSA-related infectious illnesses. There is no evidence that antibiotic use is responsible for the presence of MRSA in livestock.

seen in hospital settings and among athletes in non-sexual contexts.

CHAPTER 3   Personal Experiences with MRSA

FOREWORD

"Medicine, to produce health, has to examine disease."
—Plutarch

Independent research on a health issue is often the first step to complement discussions with a physician. But locating accurate, well-organized, understandable medical information can be a challenge. A simple Internet search on terms such as "cancer" or "diabetes," for example, returns an intimidating number of results. Sifting through the results can be daunting, particularly when some of the information is inconsistent or even contradictory. The Greenhaven Press series Perspectives on Diseases and Disorders offers a solution to the often overwhelming nature of researching diseases and disorders.

From the clinical to the personal, titles in the Perspectives on Diseases and Disorders series provide students and other researchers with authoritative, accessible information in unique anthologies that include basic information about the disease or disorder, controversial aspects of diagnosis and treatment, and first-person accounts of those impacted by the disease. The result is a well-rounded combination of primary and secondary sources that, together, provide the reader with a better understanding of the disease or disorder.

Each volume in Perspectives on Diseases and Disorders explores a particular disease or disorder in detail. Material for each volume is carefully selected from a wide range of sources, including encyclopedias, journals, newspapers, nonfiction books, speeches, government documents, pamphlets, organization newsletters, and position papers. Articles in the first chapter provide an authoritative, up-to-date overview that covers symptoms, causes and effects, treatments, cures, and medical advances. The second chapter presents a substantial number of opposing viewpoints on controversial treatments and other current debates relating to the volume topic. The third chapter offers a variety of personal perspectives on the disease or disorder. Patients, doctors, caregivers, and loved ones represent just some of the voices found in this narrative chapter.

Each Perspectives on Diseases and Disorders volume also includes:

- An **annotated table of contents** that provides a brief summary of each article in the volume.
- An **introduction** specific to the volume topic.
- Full-color **charts and graphs** to illustrate key points, concepts, and theories.
- Full-color **photos** that show aspects of the disease or disorder and enhance textual material.
- **"Fast Facts"** that highlight pertinent additional statistics and surprising points.
- A **glossary** providing users with definitions of important terms.
- A **chronology** of important dates relating to the disease or disorder.
- An annotated list of **organizations to contact** for students and other readers seeking additional information.
- A **bibliography** of additional books and periodicals for further research.
- A detailed **subject index** that allows readers to quickly find the information they need.

Whether a student researching a disorder, a patient recently diagnosed with a disease, or an individual who simply wants to learn more about a particular disease or disorder, a reader who turns to Perspectives on Diseases and Disorders will find a wealth of information in each volume that offers not only basic information, but also vigorous debate from multiple perspectives.

INTRODUCTION

On a late summer day in 2004, Christina Jones gave her husband, Marshall, a routine monthly haircut. The following day Marshall noticed an annoying ingrown hair on the back of his neck; the couple presumed it had been nicked during the haircut, and Christina plucked it out with tweezers. A few days later, however, the small bump had turned into an infected boil, prompting Marshall to have it examined by a physician. The doctor, concluding that the infection was the result of a spider bite, drained the boil and prescribed an antibiotic to aid with healing. But the boil got worse over the next several days, so Marshall returned to the doctor to have the wound reopened and some deeper layers of infection cleaned out. This time, he was given a stronger antibiotic, along with instructions to clean and redress the wound each day until it healed. A lab culture revealed that Marshall's boil was a "staph" infection—a common skin infection caused by the *Staphylococcus aureus* bacterium —but apparently it was "ordinary" staph, not the antibiotic-resistant strain that had been making headlines. Marshall and Christina were relieved to hear this news. His skin infection cleared up after another week, and the couple presumed that the ordeal was over.

They were wrong. Two months later, Marshall began experiencing back pain. Over the course of a few days, the pain became severe and was accompanied by vomiting. Fearing that he might have a kidney stone, Christina rushed Marshall to an emergency room. With a fever of 104° F and unusually high blood sugar, Marshall was put on intravenous antibiotics and given a series of scans and tests. His blood work revealed that he indeed had an invasive MRSA (methicillin-resistant *Staphylococcus aureus*) infection, and his body was in a state of septic shock. He was placed on a ventilator in a hospital intensive care unit, where he remained for two weeks until he was out of the danger zone. Afterwards, Marshall remained hospitalized for two months. MRSA had spread to different areas of his body: He had pneumonia, an infected heart valve, and internal abscesses near his spine. Because his kidneys had temporarily shut down, he had to undergo dialysis to rid his body of wastes. When he was able to return home, Marshall continued to take antibiotics for several months, and he also needed therapy for neuropathy (nerve pain) in his feet—a lingering side effect of MRSA.

Marshall fully recovered nearly a year after he first noticed the irritated bump on his neck. His illness was quite serious, and he is lucky to be alive. While most MRSA infections are not as severe as Marshall's was, the Centers for Disease Control and Prevention (CDC) reports that there are more than a hundred thousand cases of invasive MRSA in the United States each year—resulting in more than twenty thousand deaths. In many Western nations, MRSA now kills more people than AIDS.

The emergence of MRSA is one example of how seemingly miraculous medical advances can backfire. In 1928, British researcher Alexander Fleming discovered that the penicillium mold could kill staph bacteria, setting off a series of experiments and clinical trials that led to the development of the antibiotic penicillin. By the 1940s, however, a strain of *Staphylococcus aureus* had adapted by creating an enzyme that could cut through penicillin. Other antibiotics were being fashioned at this time, including methicillin, a medicine in the penicillin family that was effective against the first drug-resistant strain of *S. aureus*. But by 1960, just one year after methicillin hit the market, English bacteriologist Patricia Jevons discovered methicillin-resistant strains of *S. aureus* during her

According to the Centers for Disease Control and Prevention, more than one hundred thousand cases of invasive MRSA occur in the United States each year. (© David Nicholls/ Photo Researchers, Inc.)

research on bacterial samples. Shortly thereafter, the first MRSA infections began appearing in European and Australian hospitals.

"We can always expect antibiotic resistance to follow antibiotic use, as surely as night follows day,"[1] asserts CDC epidemiologist John Jernigan. Science reporter Jeremy Manier explains further: "Antibiotics shove bacteria into an evolutionary corner, weeding out the vulnerable varieties and offering an opportunity to strains that have picked up key defensive traits."[2] For the resistant staph bacteria, that key trait was a mutated gene known as mecA. MecA prevents methicillin and similar antibiotics from attacking the enzymes that make up the walls of the bacterial cells, thus allowing the bacteria to reproduce normally. Moreover, ordinary staph bacteria have the ability to acquire—and to spread—the resistance gene, which is what it is currently doing in today's antibiotic-rich environment. *S. aureus* can "build" resistance, transforming into MRSA if pressed to do so by the presence of antibiotics.

The staph bacterium—including MRSA—is normally found in the environment and on the human body. It typically remains harmless, but if it invades a wound or enters the body of a person with a compromised immune system, infection and illness can result. In the above-discussed case of Marshall Jones, staph bacteria became dangerous because of his undiagnosed diabetic condition; they may have also acquired drug resistance during their exposure to the antibiotics initially prescribed for him.

Today, only a few antibiotics remain effective against MRSA. One of them, vancomycin, must be given intravenously, requiring a patient to be treated in a hospital. Not surprisingly, vancomycin-resistant strains of staph—VRSA—have begun to emerge. Medical researchers continue to seek new antibiotics to combat MRSA and VRSA, but they realize that they face a great challenge, given the fast evolution of drug resistance in *S. aureus*. A vaccine for MRSA, currently under study, may prove to be more effective than antibiotics because it would prevent infection or greatly reduce its severity.

Yet another alternative to antibiotics offers hope: phage therapy. A phage (short for *bacteriophage*) is a virus that feeds on and kills bacteria without having an adverse effect on the host organism. First discovered in 1915, phages have been used in Russia and India for decades as a folk remedy for wounds. Phages were studied in the Soviet state of Georgia after World War II, but a poor understanding of their ecology and the initial success of antibiotics led Western scientists to reject them as a suitable avenue for research. Today, however, scientists are reopening serious investigations into phages. One California-based group, Phage International, has teamed with doctors at a clinic in Tbilisi, Georgia, to treat patients with antibiotic-resistant infections and claims a nearly 100 percent success rate. An India-based company, GangaGen Biotechnologies, has developed a phage-based protein known as StaphTAME. The company maintains that the protein, currently undergoing clinical trials, can kill all strains of *Staphylococcus*, including MRSA.

Phages work by attaching to bacterial cells and injecting their own DNA into them. The viral DNA takes control of the bacterial cell, stopping its vital functions and "feeding" on it in order to reproduce. A major advantage of phages is that they are selective, attacking specific strains of bacteria. Phages multiply only as long as the bacteria remain—reproducing themselves in the host's body until its "food"—the infection—is gone. In addition, many scientists purport that bacteria are not as likely to develop resistance to phages in the way that they have with antibiotics.

In the United States, phage therapy has not been approved for use in humans, although the US Food and Drug Administration has authorized phage sprays to kill *Listeria* bacteria in some food products. For now, perhaps the best weapons against MRSA and other drug-resistant bacteria are education and awareness. *Perspectives on Diseases and Disorders: MRSA* offers readers an informative overview of the emergence of MRSA, presents several current debates about how it is spread and which approaches are best for preventing and reducing infections, and shares the personal experiences of those who have struggled with MRSA-related illnesses.

Notes

1. Quoted in Jeremy Manier, "How Staph Became Drug-Resistant Threat," *Chicago Tribune*, November 4, 2007. http://articles.chicagotribune.com/2007-11-04/news/07 11030893_1_mrsa-superbug-drug-resistant.
2. Manier, "How Staph Became Drug-Resistant Threat."

CHAPTER 1

Understanding MRSA

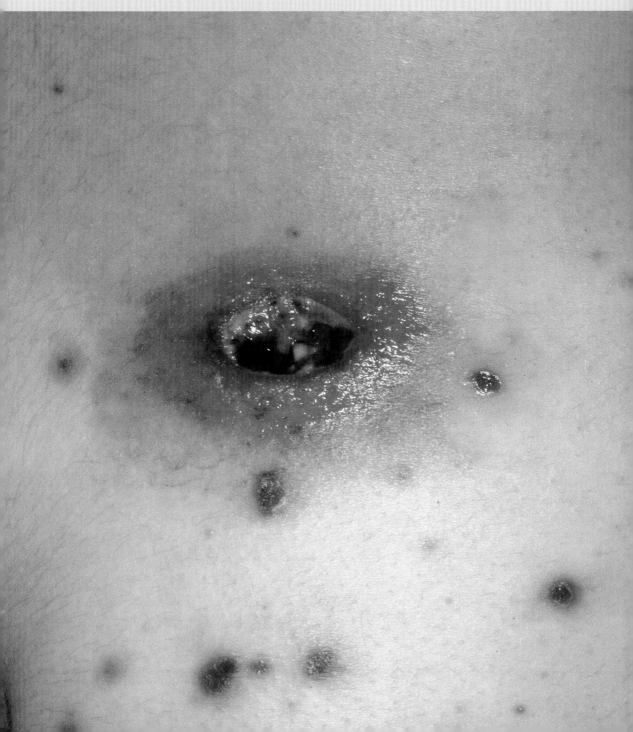

MRSA: An Overview

Brian Hoyle

In the following selection, medical writer Brian Hoyle discusses the emergence and impact of MRSA (methicillin-resistant *Staphylococcus aureus*), a bacterium that can cause a variety of severe infections. MRSA first appeared in the early 1960s, after the synthetic antibiotic methicillin had been introduced as a way to treat penicillin-resistant staph infections. This resistance, brought about by a genetic mutation within the *S. aureus* bacterium, was transmitted to other populations of staph; MRSA now exists globally. The staph bacterium (including MRSA) is normally found in the environment and typically remains harmless until it invades a wound or enters the body of a person with a compromised immune system. Hospitals and athletic facilities—where wounds are present—are known as places that can facilitate the spread of MRSA, but MRSA is also becoming more prevalent in community settings. There are a few antibiotics, such as vancomycin, that can combat MRSA, but some recent variants of the bacteria have developed resistance to it as well. Researchers are working on new antibiotics and alternative therapies, including bacteriophages—viruses designed to destroy bacteria. For now, frequent handwashing is the most effective way to help prevent the spread of MRSA.

SOURCE: Brian Hoyle, *Infectious Diseases: in Context, Vol. 1 AIDS to Lyme Disease, Vol. 2 Malaria to Zoonoses* (2-vol. set), 24E. Detroit, MI: Gale, 2008, pp. 570–572. Copyright © 2008 by Cengage Learning. All rights reserved. Reproduced by permission.

Photo on previous page. Methicillin-resistant *Staphylococcus aureus*, or MRSA, is the bacterium that causes potentially fatal infections that cannot be cured by commonly used antibiotics.
(© Scott Camazine/Photo Researchers, Inc.)

MRSa is an acronym for methicillin-resistant *Staphylococcus aureus*, which is a particular type (strain) of *S. aureus*. The bacterium is important because of its antibiotic resistance and because it can cause a number of severe diseases. One such disease is necrotizing fasciitis, more popularly known as "flesh-eating disease." MRSa is also known as oxacillin-resistant *S. aureus* (oxacillin is another antibiotic) and multiple-resistant *S. aureus*.

Until the beginning of this century, MRSa was almost exclusively found in hospitals, because the tremendous antibiotic use in hospitals provided a powerful selection pressure, that is, an environment where only the most resilient bacteria could survive. [Since] 2007, the prevalence of MRSa in environments outside of the hospital is increasing. This form of the bacterium (whether it is different from the hospital form of MRSa is not known) has been designated as community associated-MRSa or CA-MRSa.

Disease History, Characteristics, and Transmission

MRSa is resistant to methicillin, a synthetic penicillin antibiotic. It is also resistant to all of the penicillin class of antibiotics. This wide range of resistance makes the bacterium hard to treat, since commonly used antibiotics will not kill it.

MRSa has been evident almost as long as methicillin has been in use. Methicillin was introduced in 1959 to treat strains of *S. aureus* that had developed resistance to penicillin. By chemically altering the structure of penicillin, scientists were able to produce methicillin, and the penicillin-resistant *S. aureus* were killed by the newly synthesized antibiotic. But this beneficial effect did not last long. By 1961, MRSa were making a comeback, despite the use of methicillin in the United Kingdom (UK). Soon, reports of MRSa came from other countries in Europe,

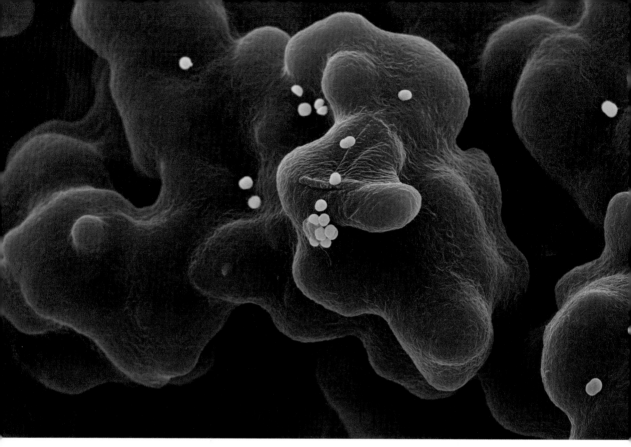

A colored electron micrograph shows methicillin-resistant *Staphylococcus aureus* (MRSA) bacteria in yellow. (© **Martin Oeggerli/Photo Researchers, Inc.**)

Japan, Australia, and North America. By 2005, thousands of hospital deaths in the UK were caused by MRSa, and the organism accounted for almost 50% of all hospital-acquired infections.

Methicillin resistance is caused by the presence of a gene (a section of genetic material that codes for the production of a protein or other compound) that codes for a protein that binds to the antibiotic and prevents the antibiotic from entering the bacteria. The *S. aureus* that is susceptible to methicillin does not have this gene. It is the transfer of this gene from one bacterium to another that has spread the resistance through populations of *Staphylococcus* around the globe.

The spread of MRSa has been aided by the fact that *S. aureus* is normally found in the environment. The bacterium is present in soil and in our bodies. Studies of the bacteria present in certain areas of the body have revealed that approximately 30% of healthy adults harbor *S. aureus*, including MRSa, on the surface of their skin or in other places, like their noses. In these environments, the bacterium is harmless. But, if MRSa gets into a wound and/or if a person's immune system is not functioning efficiently, illness can result.

MRSa is sometimes capable of causing necrotizing fasciitis, an extremely invasive disease that progresses rapidly. Sometimes amputation of the infected limb is the only way to save the patient's life. MRSa can also carry genes that code for the production of potent toxins. If these toxins get into the bloodstream, the resulting effects can be devastating to the body.

Scope and Distribution

Since *S. aureus* has a worldwide distribution, it is not surprising that MRSa has a similar distribution. In the past, MRSa was usually found in hospitals and athletic facilities, since both are places where abrasions, cuts, and scrapes occur. [Since] 2007, however, MRSa is becoming increasingly prevalent in the community, which raises the possibility that certain illnesses, such as necrotizing fasciitis, may become more common.

It is estimated that over 50 million people around the globe carry MRSa in their bodies. In the United States, about 32% of people are colonized with *S. aureus* in their noses. Colonization refers to bacteria (or other pathogens) that establish a presence on a tissue. Fewer than one percent of otherwise healthy individuals colonized with MRSa will develop a MRSa-related disease.

Having another infection can increase the likelihood of developing a MRSa infection. For example, individuals with cystic fibrosis often have recurring lung infections that require treatment with a number of different antibiotics. This situation increases the risk that MRSa will be able to gain a foothold in these patients.

MRSA Infections by Organ System and Setting

MRSA Hospital

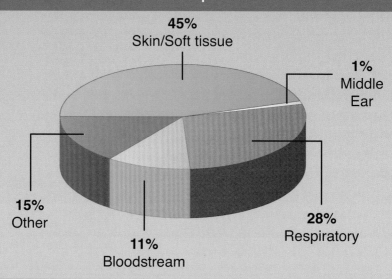

45%
Skin/Soft tissue

1%
Middle
Ear

15%
Other

11%
Bloodstream

28%
Respiratory

MRSA Community

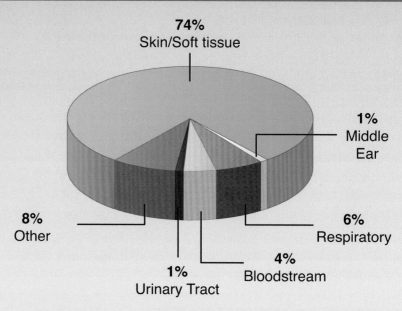

74%
Skin/Soft tissue

1%
Middle
Ear

8%
Other

1%
Urinary Tract

4%
Bloodstream

6%
Respiratory

Taken from: T.S. Naimi et al. "Comparison of Community- and Health Care–Associated Methicillin-Resistant *Staphylococcus aureaus* Infection," *Journal of the American Medical Association*, December 10, 2003.

Ominously, in February of 2007, an article appeared in *Clinical & Infectious Disease* detailing the person-to-person spread of CA-MRSa via sexual contact. This is the first time this route of transmission has been reported for MRSa.

Treatment and Prevention

Treating MRSa is challenging. Only a few antibiotics remain effective against the bacterium. One of these is vancomycin. It has the disadvantage of not being absorbed easily into the body; it cannot be given by mouth because there will be little active compound left by the time the antibiotic circulates through the bloodstream to the site of the infection. Rather, vancomycin must be given intravenously—via a needle inserted into a vein. This usually means that a person being treated must be hospitalized.

The search continues for new antibiotics that will be effective against MRSa. This research is literally a race against time. The development of new antibiotics must at least keep pace with the evolution of resistance by MRSa.

Another potential treatment option is called phage therapy. *Phage* is short for bacteriophage, which is a virus that specifically infects and forms new phage particles inside of a bacterium. The phage-bacterium association is specific—a certain type of phage infects a certain type of bacterium. In doing so, the phage ultimately destroys the bacterial cell. Scientists are experimenting with a phage that targets MRSa. If this technique proves successful, it would be a powerful treatment, since resistance to a phage does not typically develop.

Contact precautions, including handwashing, are critical in preventing MRSa infection. In a hospital, washing hands before and after caring for a patient is the most important method of preventing the spread of MRSa from

> **FAST FACT**
>
> According to the Centers for Disease Control and Prevention, two thousand to three thousand people die each year of necrotizing fasciitis—"flesh-eating disease"—which can be caused by MRSA.

patient to patient. Many hospitals now have alcohol-based hand cleansers in each room, sometimes right by each patient's bed. Washing with an alcohol-based wash takes only a few seconds, and, thus, is easier for busy health care providers to do. Moreover, MRSa is usually sensitive to alcohol. Compliance with handwashing precautions is surprisingly low. Surveys in the United States and Europe have confirmed that health care providers only wash their hands about half as much as is optimum for reducing the spread of infection. The Centers for Disease Control and Prevention has estimated that properly performed handwashing could save 30,000 lives a year that are currently lost due to hospital acquired infections, including MRSa infections.

Impacts and Issues

Studies have indicated that a hospitalized patient who acquires MRSa is about five times more likely to die than a patient in the same hospital that does not carry the bacterium.

Variants of MRSa are appearing that are resistant even to vancomycin. These new forms of the bacterium, which are called vancomycin intermediate-resistant *Staphylococcus aureus*, are especially troublesome, as they can be treated with only a very few compounds. With time, further resistance could develop, and, if newer and more powerful (and likely more expensive) antibacterial agents have not been discovered and tested, there could be no means of combating the infections.

In 2006, researchers published a paper in *Nature* describing the development of a new antibiotic produced by a fungus. This antibiotic, called platensimycin, successfully treats MRSa infections, but further preclinical studies and human clinical trials are necessary before the drug can be approved for human use.

Community-acquired MRSa is a great concern. The organism tends to more aggressively invade tissues and produces a more severe infection than that produced by hospital-acquired MRSa, for reasons that are not yet clear. In addition, it has been discovered that MRSa can grow and divide inside another microscopic organism called *Acanthamoeba*. *Acanthamoeba* can become airborne and drift for a considerable distance on air currents. This may mean that MRSa is acquiring the ability to spread great distances, which would make treatment even harder.

The Rise of Antibiotic-Resistant Infections

Mary Quirk

Nearly all significant bacterial infections affecting humans are becoming resistant to commonly prescribed antibiotics, writes Mary Quirk in the following selection. This is due to the widespread use of antibiotics over the past fifty years, which has pushed many bacteria to evolve and reproduce antibiotic-resistant variants, sometimes referred to as "superbugs." Compounding the problem is the pressure that doctors are under to prescribe antibiotics for respiratory infections involving sore throats and coughs, Quirk explains. These kinds of infections are usually caused by cold or flu viruses, which are not killed by antibiotics. When antibiotics are used for viral infections, they can kill beneficial bacteria that help to keep antibiotic-resistant bacteria under control—and thereby allow the population of resistant bacteria to multiply. Experts note that many bacterial infections actually get better on their own; thus, physicians need to be more discerning about prescribing antibiotics. Quirk is a medical and science writer who has contributed numerous articles to medical journals, including *The Lancet* and *Clinical Infectious Diseases*.

SOURCE: Mary Quirk, "Antibiotic-Resistant Infections," *Diseases and Disorders,* vol. 1. Tarrytown, NY: Marshall Cavendish, 2008. Copyright © 2008 by Marshall Cavendish Corporation. All rights reserved. Reproduced by permission.

Antibiotics were discovered in the 1940s and have been used to successfully treat infections caused by bacteria. For decades, these miracle drugs have prevented serious illness and death from bacterial diseases. Unfortunately, antibiotic use also promotes the development of antibiotic-resistant bacteria. According to the U.S. Centers for Disease Control and Prevention (CDC), almost all significant bacterial infections affecting humans are becoming resistant to commonly prescribed antibiotics.

Doctors can no longer rely on their first or second choice of antibiotics to fight many human infections. Scientists are concerned that physicians will lose these essential infection-fighting tools. The majority of the most serious antibiotic-resistant infections occur in hospitalized people, but these infections are becoming more frequent in healthy people. Public health officials are sounding the alarm about antibiotic resistance because of the emergence of "superbugs" in the last decade. These germs are resistant to many antibiotics, including powerful drugs such as vancomycin, which is reserved by physicians to fight the most stubborn infections.

"Germs in a Hospital Ward" cartoon by Graham Chaffer, www.Cartoon Stock.com. Copyright © Graham Chaffer. Reproduction rights obtainable from www.CartoonStock.com.

Microbe Wars

Antibiotic-resistant infections are caused by bacteria that survive treatment with commonly prescribed antibiotics. When bacteria reproduce, slight changes occur in their genetic material. Some of these changes allow bacteria to evade certain antibiotics.

Each person carries more microorganisms on the skin than there are people in the world. Bacteria that coexist on our skin and in our bodies without causing disease are called healthy bacterial flora. When antibiotic-resistant bacteria develop, they compete with our own flora, becoming a trivial member of our bacterial melting pot. However, in the presence of an antibiotic drug, the resistant bacteria can magnify their population a thousandfold to a millionfold. The resulting infection is harder to treat and often requires a more powerful antibiotic drug.

Both viruses and bacteria cause common infections. However, antibiotics fight only those infections caused by bacteria, not those caused by viruses. Viruses and bacteria are distinct. Bacteria are one of the smallest life-forms and occur as single cells. Many bacteria are not harmful, and some are actually beneficial. Disease-causing bacteria can grow on the skin or inside the body and cause illness. For example, strep throat is caused by bacteria called *Streptococcus pyrogenes*.

Viruses are even smaller than bacteria. They are mostly genetic material—DNA or RNA—and often have a protective coat surrounding their genes. A virus cannot reproduce outside the body's cells. Viruses invade healthy cells. They use the machinery of the body's cells to make copies of themselves. Typically, newly formed viruses destroy the cell as they leave it to infect new cells. Viruses rather than bacteria are the more frequent culprits of res-

> **FAST FACT**
>
> The journal *Medical Laboratory Observer* notes that 75 percent of antibiotics are prescribed for acute respiratory-tract infections, despite the fact that 80 percent of these infections are of viral origin.

piratory illnesses such as colds, sore throats, and coughs. Most stuffy noses are caused by viruses called rhinoviruses.

Doctors Feel Pressure

During the early days of a cold or upper respiratory infection, the nose produces clear mucus. The mucus helps wash the germs from the sinuses (air-filled spaces in the skull) and nose. Immune cells then join in to fight the infection, and the mucus changes from clear to a whitish or yellowish color. During recovery from a stuffy nose, the bacteria that live normally in the nose grow back, which can change the mucus to a greenish color, which experts say is normal.

According to the CDC, doctors feel pressure to prescribe antibiotics for respiratory infections. Respiratory infections such as sore throat, cold, and coughs are usually caused by viruses. Tens of millions of antibiotics prescribed in doctors' offices are for viral infections. Using antibiotics for a viral infection offers no benefit to the affected person and could possibly cause harm. Taking unnecessary antibiotics increases the risk of antibiotic resistance developing in bacteria.

Varieties of Staph Bacteria

Staphylococcus aureus, commonly called staph bacteria, is found on human skin and in the nose. Staph bacteria are one of the most common causes of skin infections in the United States. Most of these skin infections are minor. However, staph bacteria can also cause serious blood infections and pneumonia, which can be fatal. Hospitalized patients are particularly at risk for antibiotic-resistant infections, including infections caused by staph bacteria. Often, these infections are introduced by urinary or intravenous catheters, and can be serious. Certain underlying health conditions increase the risk of infection. Such

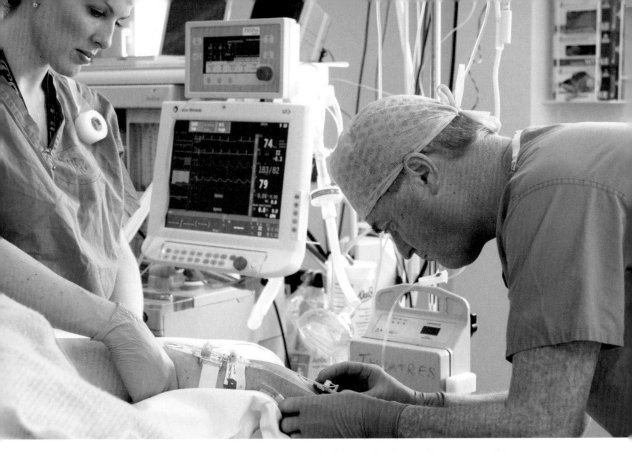

A surgical patient is anesthetized using an intravenous catheter. Hospitalized patients are at risk for antibiotic-resistant staph infections introduced by urinary and intravenous catheters. (© Life in View/Photo Researchers, Inc.)

conditions include diabetes, kidney disease, and immune-system problems. Also, antibiotic use—for example, to prevent infection after surgery—increases a patient's risk of developing a resistant infection. Staph superbugs are often referred to by their abbreviations: for example, MRSA (methicillin-resistant *Staphylococcus aureus*), VRSA (vancomycin-resistant *Staphylococcus aureus*), and VISA (vancomycin-intermediate *Staphylococcus aureus*). MRSA infections are becoming more common in various communities and are affecting healthy people. No longer confined to health care settings, MRSA outbreaks have occurred among children, athletes, and military recruits.

In the last decade, doctors are seeing more cases of antibiotic-resistant infections in healthy adults and children. Close contact with people who have antibiotic-resistant infections is an important risk factor in healthy people. In one outbreak among high school athletes, sharing of towels, sports equipment, and uniforms were important factors in transmitting MRSA from one athlete to another.

The use of antibiotics in livestock on farms is also under scrutiny by government agencies. There appears to be a link to the development of antibiotic resistance in humans, especially when the same class of drugs (for example, fluoroquinolones) are used both in livestock and to treat humans.

Preventing Antibiotic-Resistant Infections

To help prevent antibiotic-resistant infections, antibiotics should be taken as prescribed by a health care provider. A course of antibiotics should not be stopped at the first sign of improvement. To help prevent resistant bacteria from gaining an upper hand, it is very important to take every dose of the prescribed antibiotic until it is finished. Antibiotics should not be saved for use at a later time.

Experts on the subject of infections maintain that many bacterial infections get better on their own and that physicians should only prescribe antibiotics when it is likely to benefit the patient. Viral infections, such as cold or flu, do not respond to antibiotics.

Frequent hand washing is one of the easiest ways to reduce transmission of infectious diseases. Sometimes an antibiotic is needed. A health care provider should be consulted if a respiratory illness gets worse or lasts a long time. To treat an antibiotic-resistant infection, clinicians perform laboratory tests to find the antibiotic or combination of drugs that will beat the superbug. Providing clinicians with better tools to distinguish a viral illness from a bacterial infection will help prevent unnecessary antibiotic use.

MRSA Infections Are Increasing Among Teenagers

Denise Rinaldo

A growing number of young people in the United States are contract-ing MRSA infections, reports Denise Rinaldo in the following article. Until recently, MRSA typically infected patients in hospitals and nurs-ing homes, but now it is increasingly seen in athletes, military re-cruits, and children. The term for MRSA infections that occur outside of health care settings is community-acquired MRSA, or CA-MRSA, which now account for about 15 percent of new MRSA cases. These cases often begin as a minor skin infection that can be treated when caught early. But if the bacteria enter the bloodstream, they can spread to other parts of the body and cause serious illness, Rinaldo explains. Teens are advised to wash frequently, avoid sharing athletic equipment with others, and to see a doctor if they discover a painful red bump on their skin. Rinaldo is an author of books for children and young adults.

SOURCE: Denise Rinaldo, "Bug on the Loose? It's Tough to Kill It. . . . Should You Worry About the Germ Known as MRSA?," *Scholastic Choices*, vol. 24, no. 2, October 2008, p. 16. Copyright © 2008 by Scholastic Inc. All rights reserved. Reprinted by permission of the publisher.

Ryan Dowling felt lousy. His muscles ached and his energy level was low. "I figured it was from practicing baseball because I had just done tryouts," the teen from Lake Fenton, Michigan, tells *Choices*. "But I kept feeling worse."

A talented athlete who played football, hockey, and baseball, Ryan had a reputation of never complaining about any aches and pains he experienced while playing sports. Soon, though, Ryan's hip was hurting so much that he couldn't walk without crutches. His parents took him to doctors.

Blood tests revealed that Ryan's hip was infected with a potentially deadly bacterium known as MRSA (pronounced *mersa*): methicillin-resistant *Staphylococcus aureus*. Ryan had never heard of the germ.

Dangerous Route

MRSA almost always starts as a skin infection—which can be treated easily. But the bloodstream can carry an infection to other parts of the body. "Once it gets into the bloodstream, it can travel to your heart, your lungs, or anywhere else," says Jeff Hageman, an epidemiologist with the U.S. Centers for Disease Control and Prevention. "When it spreads, it can become severe, and in some cases lead to death."

Ryan recovered from his MRSA infection, but only after a grueling month in the hospital, where he underwent drug treatments and multiple surgeries. A growing number of teenagers across the United States are developing MRSA infections. Many of them are athletes, like Ryan. The key to avoiding MRSA is understanding the bug and how it works, and catching infections early, before they become as serious as Ryan's.

MRSA is a type of staph infection. *Staphyloccus aureus*, commonly called staph, is a common germ. If doctors were to test an average group of young people in the U.S.,

Many teenagers who participate in athletics are developing MRSA infections, due to the increased incidence of bodily contact and the sharing of equipment. (© Ty Downing/Workbook Stock/Getty Images)

about 30 percent of them would be colonized with staph. That means it is living in their bodies, but not causing an infection.

A Drug-Resistant Germ

What is unique about MRSA? "It is a specific type of staph that has learned to be resistant to the most common antibiotics we use to treat things like strep throat and ear infections," says Dr. Buddy Creech, a MRSA expert who is an associate professor of pediatric infectious diseases at Monroe Carell Jr. Children's Hospital at Vanderbilt University in Nashville, Tennessee. About 10 percent of young people are colonized (not infected) with MRSA, according to Creech.

Because it has built-in defenses against penicillin and related drugs, a MRSA infection is tough to treat. But it is not a superbug—a germ that no medicine can vanquish. "We've developed new drugs that should buy us time to come up with better ways to prevent and treat MRSA," Creech says.

MRSA is setting off alarm bells now because it is showing up more often in healthy young people like Ryan. Until recently, MRSA mainly infected patients in hospitals and nursing homes—those with open wounds and weak immune systems. When MRSA started turning up in people who hadn't had contact with the healthcare system, researchers came up with a new name for it: community-acquired MRSA (CA-MRSA). Now, about 15 percent of new MRSA cases are CA-MRSA.

At-Risk Groups

Who is at the highest risk for CA-MRSA? Children, military recruits, and athletes like Ryan. People in all those groups get a lot of cuts and scrapes, and spend a lot of time in close contact with others. The touching, pushing, and sharing of equipment that are common among athletes make it easy for MRSA to spread from one person's skin to another's. The cuts and scrapes give the germs a place to enter the body and cause infection. About 14,000 cases of serious CA-MRSA were diagnosed in the U.S. in 2005, the most recent year for which figures are available.

FAST FACT

Between 1999 and 2008, the number of children hospitalized for MRSA increased tenfold, according to the journal *Pediatrics*.

Ryan doesn't know how MRSA entered his body. He doesn't remember any cuts or a skin infection. "My doctor thinks I probably got a deep bruise near my hip playing hockey, the germ somehow got into my blood, and it traveled from there," Ryan says.

Ryan does know, however, how to cut down the chance of getting MRSA. "Keep your body clean and make sure you don't borrow other people's equipment," he says.

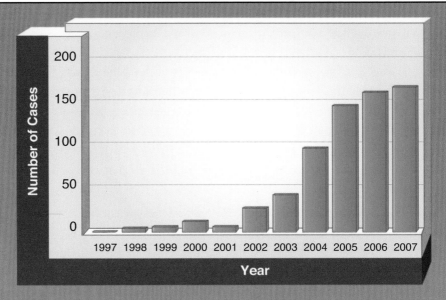

MRSA Incidence at Seattle Children's Hospital

Taken from: *ScienceBlogs*, "Discovering Biology in a Digital World," www.scienceblogs.com.

The most common symptom of MRSA skin infection is a painful and pus-filled boil or pimple. "Often people describe it as looking like a spider bite," Hageman says. If you have a suspicious red bump anywhere on your body, it is important to see a doctor to be checked for MRSA.

"It's common for skin infections to occur at sites on the body that may be uncomfortable to tell your parents about, such as the groin or the armpit," Hageman says. If that happens to you, it's important to tell your parents, even if it might be embarrassing to do so.

Serious Symptoms

People with more advanced MRSA infections often develop high fevers. MRSA bone infections, like the one Ryan had, are characterized by joint or bone pain. "Call a doctor if you have an unexplained pain or fever, or if it hurts to put weight on your leg—especially if you've recently had a skin infection," Creech says. "Anytime you get sick shortly after having a skin infection, mention the infection to your doctor."

When Ryan came home from the hospital, his infection was cured, but much had changed. His weight had dropped from 158 to 122 pounds. He still needed crutches to walk. Sports, which had been the center of Ryan's life, were out of the question. Later, doctors discovered that MRSA had totally destroyed Ryan's hip. "His leg bone was two inches higher than it should be," says Ryan's father, Greg Dowling. "The infection had totally blown through his hip socket."

In August 2007, Ryan returned to the hospital for hip replacement surgery. Doctors removed what was left of his old hip joint and replaced it with an artificial one. "From the day after the hip replacement surgery, it felt really good," Ryan says. "I had more movement that day than I had since I got MRSA."

The athlete is making a comeback. Last school year [2007], Ryan played a little hockey and was able to play baseball. This year [2008], his senior year, he is hoping to suit up for football.

Despite what he has been through, Ryan is thankful. "I feel really lucky," he says. "I just hope nobody else has to go through what I experienced."

The Search for
a MRSA Vaccine

University of Chicago Medical Center

The following press release from the University of Chicago Medical Center offers an overview of the challenges involved in developing a MRSA vaccine and looks at two new approaches that offer hope. One significant challenge is the ability of *Staphylococcus aureus* to suppress the immune system long enough for it to settle into body tissues and spread to other parts of the body. A vaccine could emerge from the genetic manipulation of the staph bacterium's cell-surface proteins in such a way that would enable the immune system to launch an effective attack. Another approach would interrupt MRSA's ability to develop protected niches within body tissues. Current studies are testing a potential vaccine that would combine both of these approaches.

Two recent studies provide evidence for a new approach to vaccines to prevent infections caused by drug-resistant *Staphylococcus aureus*—better known

SOURCE: University of Chicago Medical Center, "Studies Pinpoint Key Targets for MRSA Vaccine," news release, August 16, 2010. www .uchospitals.edu. Courtesy of the University of Chicago Medical Center.

as MRSA—the leading cause of skin and soft tissue, bloodstream and lung infections in the United States. One demonstrates a way to counteract the bacteria's knack for evading the immune system. The other shows how to disrupt the germ's tissue-damaging mechanism.

Each approach dramatically reduced the virulence of staph infections in mice. The combination may protect people from MRSA infections and provide lasting immunity to this virulent and drug-resistant organism, which has become the leading cause of death from infectious disease in the United States.

Challenges of Creating a Staph Vaccine

Since the 1960s, development of a staph vaccine has been a priority for the medical profession—but less so for the pharmaceutical industry, which has veered away from vaccine research. Previous attempts at a MRSA vaccine have failed. In the last decade, however, as staph increased its ability to resist multiple antibiotics and drug-resistant strains came to dominate the community setting, the search for a protective vaccine has moved to center stage.

One of the challenges in creating a vaccine is the ability of this germ to short-circuit the host's defenses. Most bacterial infections trigger an immune counter-attack designed to rid the body of the microbe and prevent subsequent infections. Most vaccines rely on this same strategy. Staph, however, has evolved its own tools to blunt the immune response.

"Staph aureus is the world champion of immune suppression," said the senior author of both studies, Olaf Schneewind, PhD, professor and chair of microbiology at the University of Chicago. This allows the organism to persist long enough to escape the blood stream and settle into various tissues, where it builds a protective capsule, replicates and soon spreads in greater numbers to additional sites.

"Even when the infection can be cleared with antibiotics and surgery, the patient has no immunity," he said. "So these infections often recur."

Targeting Proteins

An effective vaccine requires finding the right targets: proteins key to the disease process and exposed on the cell surface. Schneewind and colleague Dominique Missiakas, PhD, associate professor of microbiology at the University, began by assembling a library of all 23 surface proteins made by staph and created new strains with a mutated version of each protein. So each strain was normal except for one disabled surface protein. When they exposed mice to these mutant microbes, two sets of potential vaccine targets emerged.

> **FAST FACT**
>
> A Vanderbilt University study found that staph has evolved to target human hemoglobin so it can burst red blood cells open and feed on the iron inside.

One, known as protein A, is a cell-surface molecule than binds to receptors on B cells, the white blood cells that produce antibodies. Protein A is the key to staph's ability to evade immunity. It shields the bacteria by "cross-linking" two receptors on the B cells. This triggers cell death. So mice confronted with a staph infection do not make antibodies against the bacteria.

In the August 17, 2010, issue of the *Journal of Experimental Medicine*, Schneewind's team tested a way around that obstacle. They found that staph with a mutant version of protein A, unable to short-circuit B cells, did stimulate an immune response. Mice exposed to the "non-toxic" version of protein A were able to mount an effective immune response, killing bacteria—including the virulent strain known as USA300, the current source of about 60 percent of staph infections. The vaccine enabled these mice to reduce tissue damage and prevent, or at least delay, death.

"I believe," said Schneewind, "that protein A may be the key to making a staphylococcal vaccine."

How Vaccines and Antibodies Work

While some vaccines use different methods, this illustration shows how most vaccines work.

A weakened form of the disease germ is injected into the body.

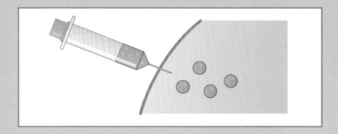

The body makes antibodies to fight these invaders.

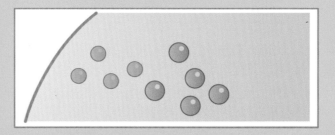

If the actual disease germs ever attack the body, the antibodies will still be there to destroy them.

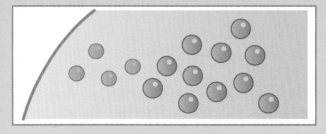

Taken from: Centers for Disease Control and Prevention, "How Vaccines Prevent Disease," August 7, 2009. www.cdc.gov.

Destroying Bacterial Niches

The second target was a set of two clotting factors, coagulase and von Willebrand factor binding protein (vWbp), that the bacteria use to assemble protected niches within various tissues where they can replicate.

When the bacteria leave the bloodstream, they settle into various organs, such as the kidneys. In this setting, they use these clotting factors to build a protected environment, called an abscess, where they can multiply. After several days, these abscesses rupture, spilling a new load of

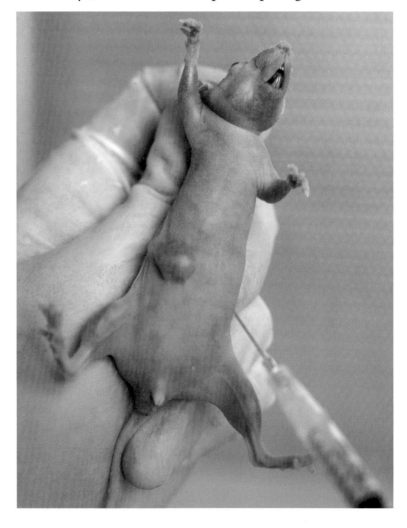

Lab mice that were inoculated with an anticoagulase vaccine had far fewer abscesses and survived longer after infection with MRSA. (©Hank Morgan/ Photo Researchers, Inc.)

bacteria into the bloodstream where they can disseminate to uninfected tissues.

Bacteria that lacked functional versions of these two clotting factors were unable to form abscesses or persist in infected tissues. In the August 2010 issue of *PLoS Pathogens*, Schneewind and colleagues show that by generating antibodies to these two clotting factors and transferring them to infected mice, they could protect those mice from a staph infection.

They also made and tested an anti-coagulase vaccine by injecting purified versions of the clotting factors from a different kind of bacteria (*E. coli*) into mice and allowing the mice time to produce antibodies. About two weeks later they injected the mice with staph. Even when injected with the USA300, mice vaccinated with both antigens had far fewer abscesses and survived longer.

"The establishment of abscess lesions can be blocked with antibodies specific for coagulases," the authors conclude. "These data further corroborate the concept that Coagulase and vWbp should be considered for staphylococcal vaccine development."

Studies testing the ability of a vaccine combining both approaches are under way.

CHAPTER 2

Controversies Concerning MRSA

Overuse of Antibiotics on Factory Farms Has Allowed MRSA to Enter the Food Supply

Ian Lordon

The livestock production industry is a major contributor to the increase in antibiotic-resistant bacteria, contends Ian Lordon in the following viewpoint. Most notably, the increase in MRSA infections over the past two decades corresponds with the reliance on large factory farms (rather than small family farms) for meat production. Factory farms give antibiotic feed additives to cows, pigs, chickens, and other livestock to prevent the illnesses that would otherwise occur in the crowded, filthy conditions in which they are kept, Lordon explains. Because the feed additives contain low, subtherapeutic levels of antibiotics, factory farms are basically exposing microbes to doses that are insufficient to kill them off completely—which enables them to develop resistance. MRSA and other resistant bacteria are now more frequently found in the food supply, increasing the opportunity for serious bacterial infections to emerge in community settings. Lordon is the communications and outreach officer for Beyond Factory Farming, an organization promoting socially responsible livestock production in Canada.

SOURCE: Ian Lordon, "Breeding Disease: Antibiotic Resistance in Factory Farms," *Briarpatch*, vol. 39, no. 5, September/October, 2010, p. 26. Copyright © 2010 by Briarpatch Magazine. All rights reserved. Reproduced by permission.

Photo on facing page. The increase in MRSA infections in the United States corresponds with the transformation of meat production from small family farms to large factory farms. (David R. Frazier/Photo Researchers, Inc.)

Many Canadians first learned of flesh-eating disease, or necrotizing fasciitis, in 1994 when then-Bloc Québécois [political party] leader Lucien Bouchard lost his leg, and very nearly his life, to the affliction. Media reports of Bouchard's brush with death described the disease as "extremely rare." It was at the time, but has since become more commonplace. Up until 1994 there were only about 40 cases of necrotizing fasciitis recorded worldwide, while today between 90 and 200 cases are reported in Canada alone every year.

Curiously, the explanation for the sudden and remarkable rise in the number of patients suffering from flesh-eating disease may in large part lie in the very flesh we eat, bred by our livestock industry. Recent research suggests this system is a major contributor to the recent rise in antibiotic-resistant bacteria plaguing our hospitals. And these bacteria, although not traditionally associated with flesh-eating disease, are now blamed for a growing percentage of cases.

Necrotizing Fasciitis

What is flesh-eating disease?

Flesh-eating disease doesn't actually consume flesh; rather, it kills flesh when toxins produced by bacteria destroy skin and muscle. If left untreated, the infection will spread to the bloodstream, leading to organ failure and often death within days. Because of the toxicity and rapid onset of the disease, treatment generally involves surgical removal of the infected flesh and the administration of antibiotics intravenously.

In the case of Bouchard, diagnosis and treatment came too late to save his leg, but was at least able to save his life.

Historically, most cases of flesh-eating disease developed in patients with weakened immune systems who fell prey to *Streptococcus* infections acquired in hospital. Since 2001, however, hospitals have increasingly reported incidents of flesh-eating disease brought on by methicillin-resistant *Staphylococcus aureus* (MRSA) infections—bacteria able to resist traditional antibiotic treatments.

An Increase in MRSA Infections

This should come as no surprise, as the number of reported MRSA infections has increased enormously over the last 20 years in lockstep with a corresponding transformation in livestock production from small family farms to large-scale factory farms ushered in first by the Canada-U.S. Free Trade Agreement in 1989, and later bolstered by NAFTA [North American Free Trade Agreement] in 1994. Researchers with the Canadian Nosocomial Infection Surveillance Program released a survey in March [2010] that found reported cases of patients infected or colonized by MRSA in Canadian hospitals increased 17-fold between 1995 and 2007. Today in the

Necrotizing fasciitis cases have been on the rise in Canada. The flesh-eating disease is resistant to antibiotic treatment. (© **Dr. M.A. Ansary/Photo Researchers, Inc.**)

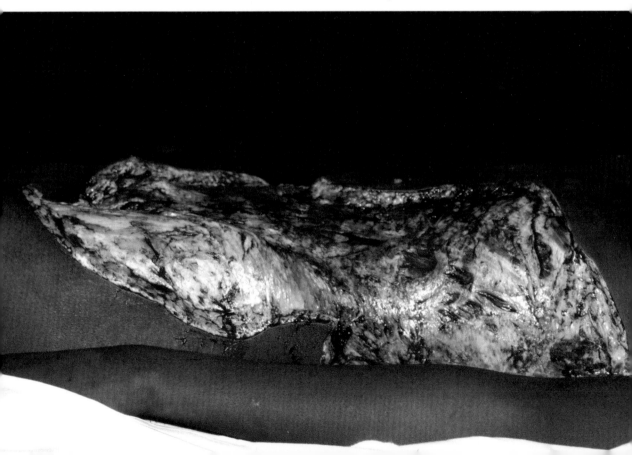

US the lives of more than 18,000 people are claimed by MRSA-related infection every year, exceeding AIDS-related deaths.

The vast majority of MRSA infections, however, are not fatal. Patients merely develop boils, sometimes accompanied by a fever or rash, that can be treated effectively, albeit expensively, with recently developed antibiotics. However, pneumonia, widespread infection and toxic shock syndrome can also result from more virulent strains.

MRSA infections inevitably tax limited health care resources and jeopardize patient care. The Public Health Agency of Canada estimated direct health care costs attributable to MRSA at $82 million in 2004 and predicted the total would rise to $129 million by 2010.

Researchers have divided the many strains of antibiotic-resistant bacteria into two groups: community-associated and hospital-associated. As their names suggest, hospital-associated strains are those that originate within health care facilities, while community-associated strains originate outside. Community-associated MRSA strains are generally more virulent, more dangerous and until recently, occurred much less frequently. In 1995, community-associated MRSA strains accounted for just six per cent of reported cases in Canada, rising to 23 per cent by 2007. Now, recent estimates have the figure as high as 40 per cent. Worse, many of these more virulent strains have now established themselves in hospitals and other health care facilities. Among the elderly, sick and vulnerable, they are exceedingly difficult to eradicate.

"It is still mostly a hospital-acquired infection," Dr. Andrew Simor, chief of microbiology and infectious diseases at the Sunnybrook Health Sciences Centre in Toronto, told the CBC [Canadian Broadcasting Corporation] recently. Over the past five years, MRSA infections in children and young adults outside hospitals have dramatically increased, he explained.

"We need to continue to be vigilant in controlling this infection and developing more effective interventions to control the rapid emergence of more virulent community-associated MRSA strains from the community that have now been introduced into hospital settings in Canada."

Health care professionals, policymakers and researchers are understandably alarmed by this trend and keen to identify its source. Recent research aimed at explaining it is pointing the finger at factory farms.

Resistance on the Rise

When Alexander Fleming was awarded the Nobel prize in 1945 for his part in discovering penicillin, the first antibiotic, he remarked that it was easy to produce microbes resistant to it: simply expose them to doses insufficient to kill them. This is now standard operating procedure at every factory farm in North America.

Cows, pigs, chickens and other livestock consume roughly 70 per cent of all antibiotics manufactured in the U.S.—an estimated 12 million kilograms per year. Canadian statistics are not maintained but likely closely reflect U.S. numbers because, thanks to NAFTA, agricultural practices here are largely the same. This antibiotic regime is called "subtherapeutic" because it is not administered to treat disease, but rather to prevent it. As a result, crowded, filthy conditions that would otherwise result in disease outbreaks and unacceptable losses for producers have instead become the norm.

"These are feed additives. It's like using antibiotics as hair dye," Ellen Silbergeld, a professor of environmental health sciences at the Bloomberg School of Public Health and one of several researchers at Johns Hopkins University studying the links between industrial agriculture and resistant microbes, explained to the *Baltimore Chronicle* last year [2009]. "Our food safety system is a shambles. This is a situation that is widely recognized by the World

Health Organization, the American Medical Association, and by others, and nothing happens!"

It's a model of Darwinian selection for stronger and more resistant bacteria on a massive scale. And there is a growing body of evidence suggesting that the anticipated result is in fact occurring with sobering consequences for human health.

The Link with Livestock Production

Here in Canada, the connection between resistant microbes and industrial livestock production was first documented in a 2007 study published in *Veterinary Microbiology* that examined the incidence of MRSA in pig farms in Ontario. The study reported MRSA at 45 per cent of farms sampled and in a quarter of the pigs.

Evidence linking the spread of MRSA to industrial agriculture is accumulating rapidly. The *Veterinary Microbiology* report came on the heels of a study that found Dutch pig farmers were 760 times more likely to be MRSA carriers than the public at large and a *Scientific American* report that found that 12 per cent of pork on supermarket shelves in Holland tested positive for MRSA. Also in 2007, a Centers for Disease Control and Prevention study demonstrated that a strain of MRSA originating from one animal reservoir was responsible for 20 per cent of all MRSA cases in Holland. More recently, a study in Iowa revealed similar numbers to those documented in the Ontario report: 45 per cent of farmers and 49 per cent of pigs tested positive for MRSA.

The increasing occurrence of resistant bacteria is far from limited to MRSA and hog production. Subtherapeutic use of antibiotics in cattle, dairy, hog, poultry, egg and other livestock is contributing to antibiotic resistance among microbes such as *Salmonella*, *C. difficile*, pneumonia, *E. coli* and many others.

Six years ago the World Health Organization reported that the evidence clearly linked dangerously resistant bacteria

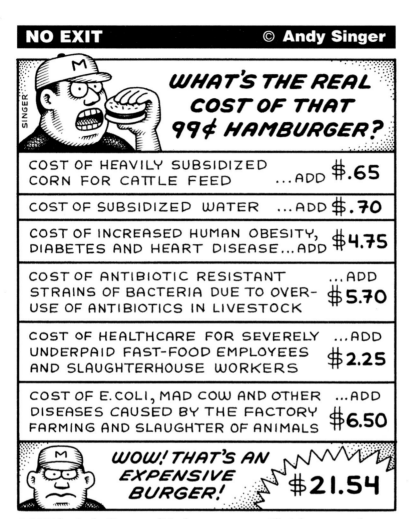

NO EXIT © **Andy Singer**

WHAT'S THE REAL COST OF THAT 99¢ HAMBURGER?

COST OF HEAVILY SUBSIDIZED CORN FOR CATTLE FEED ...ADD	$.65
COST OF SUBSIDIZED WATER ...ADD	$.70
COST OF INCREASED HUMAN OBESITY, DIABETES AND HEART DISEASE...ADD	$4.75
COST OF ANTIBIOTIC RESISTANT STRAINS OF BACTERIA DUE TO OVER-USE OF ANTIBIOTICS IN LIVESTOCK ...ADD	$5.70
COST OF HEALTHCARE FOR SEVERELY UNDERPAID FAST-FOOD EMPLOYEES AND SLAUGHTERHOUSE WORKERS ...ADD	$2.25
COST OF E.COLI, MAD COW AND OTHER DISEASES CAUSED BY THE FACTORY FARMING AND SLAUGHTER OF ANIMALS ...ADD	$6.50

WOW! THAT'S AN EXPENSIVE BURGER! $21.54

to non-human use of antimicrobials and called the situation "a crisis which threatens to rob the world of opportunities to treat or cure many infectious diseases." It also recommended governments legislate an end to non-therapeutic administration of antibiotics in agriculture. In 2006, the European Union adopted a ban on the practice.

Canada's Policy Vacuum

Meanwhile, in Canada, despite escalating health care costs and complications from antibiotic resistant microbes and the increasing ineffectiveness of many classes of traditional antibiotics, there is no such ban in place and none under consideration. In fact, in 2009 the federal government disbanded the 10-year-old Canadian Committee on Antibiotic Resistance and has ignored pleas from health experts and scientists to establish a Canadian Centre for Antimicrobial Resistance.

Since 2002, the Public Health Agency of Canada, however, has funded the Canadian Integrated Program for Antimicrobial Resistance Surveillance (CIPARS), charged with tracking antimicrobial-resistant bacteria in food and on farms, to the tune of $3 million annually. The program has competently fulfilled its mandate, yet even when the data gathered by CIPARS identifies agricultural practices that are likely contributing to antibiotic resistance, government agencies charged with intervention—Health Canada, the Public Health Agency of Canada and the Canadian Food Inspection Agency—have proven unwilling or unable to act decisively.

FAST FACT

Cooking kills MRSA, but a person with a cut on the finger, for example, could contract an infection from touching MRSA-infected raw meat.

Take the case of the widespread and unapproved use of cephalosporin antibiotics by Canadian chicken hatcheries that, according to CIPARS, was likely responsible for a rise in human resistance to that class of antibiotics. CIPARS looked specifically at Ceftiofur—an antibiotic that hatcheries were injecting into eggs to prevent future infection outbreaks among chickens. The practice, designated "off-label" because it never received formal approval by Health Canada, was suspected to be responsible for increased resistance to cephalosporin antibiotics in humans. In 2005, resistance levels in Quebec were so high that hatcheries in the province agreed to voluntarily suspend Ceftiofur injections. Within months CIPARS noted a 60 per cent decline in resistance among hatchery birds, a 30 per cent decline among samples of chicken sold at supermarkets and a 45 per cent decline in human resistance.

"The CIPARS data appears to be answering the question about a linkage between usage of antibiotics in animals and human resistance," Jim Hutchinson, chair of the Canadian Committee on Antibiotic Resistance remarked to the *Canadian Medical Association Journal* in July 2009—just days before the Public Health Agency announced it was disbanding his organization by cancelling its $300,000 annual budget.

Other researchers interpreted the CIPARS data more succinctly. "Taken in context with all the other knowledge we have, anyone still opposing a link between antibiotic use in food animal production and direct human health impact does so for other reasons than science," Frank Aarestrup, a specialist on antibiotic resistance with the Technical University of Denmark, told the *Canadian Medical Association Journal* last year [2009].

A Toothless Response

And how did Health Canada respond when presented with the evidence? It added an unenforceable warning against off-label usage to Ceftiofur packaging. Soon after, a *Canadian Medical Association Journal* report confirmed that the off-label practice of routinely injecting eggs with Ceftiofur continues in Quebec, Ontario and British Columbia today. Recent reports from CIPARS have noted that poultry, retail chicken and human resistance to cephalosporin antibiotics is on the rise once again.

The toothless response from regulators suggests that while they are willing to concede the point that agricultural use of antibiotics presents human health concerns, the health of Canadian people is less important than the perceived competitive advantage antibiotics offer to the nation's industrial livestock producers.

Ironically, Sweden, Denmark and other countries have demonstrated that if overcrowding is reduced and infection control techniques are implemented, abandoning subtherapeutic antibiotic regimes in livestock production has little, if any, impact on the bottom line. In the wake of Sweden's 1986 ban on antibiotics, the net increase in cost to consumers was estimated at 12 cents per kilo for retail meat. In Denmark, the World Health Organization reported that as of 2003, the net costs associated with productivity losses incurred by removing antimicrobial growth promoters from pig and poultry production were an estimated 1.04 [euros] per pig produced, with zero net cost for poultry. This translates into an increase in pig production costs of slightly more than one per cent.

Is 12 cents a kilo too much to pay to help maintain the life-saving potential of antibiotics? Thanks to this extraordinary but delicate class of medication, cures for tuberculosis, scarlet fever, diphtheria, syphilis, gonorrhea, meningitis and dozens of other diseases and infections that have plagued humanity for centuries now exist. Are we willing to invite a return to the days when tuberculosis alone killed one in every four people in the western hemisphere for the sake of a slightly cheaper pork chop?

The Presence of MRSA in Farm Animals Is Not Proven to Cause MRSA Infections in Humans

Cliff Gauldin

In the following viewpoint, Cliff Gauldin acknowledges that MRSA bacteria have become more prevalent in pigs, pig farmers, pork producers, and swine veterinarians in recent years. But, he contends, those who work in the pork industry do not have a higher incidence of MRSA infections than the general public does. People who carry MRSA in their nasal passages or on their skin do not necessarily get sick from it, experts point out. Moreover, representatives from the National Pork Board have found no evidence that the presence of MRSA in pigs has any connection to the use of antibiotics in their feed, as some critics have asserted. Consumer groups that hope to impose restrictions on the use of antibiotics in agriculture are using public concern about MRSA-related illnesses as a scare tactic to further their agenda, the author reports. After twenty years in the news media as a radio reporter, Gauldin has been involved with agriculture-related communications and public relations since 1994.

SOURCE: Cliff Gauldin, "Industry Taking MRSA Seriously," *Feedstuffs*, vol. 80, no. 31, August 4, 2008, p. 12. Copyright © 2008 by Feedstuffs. All rights reserved. Reproduced by permission.

The prevalence of antibiotic-resistant bacteria known as methicillin-resistant *Staphylococcus aureus* (MRSA) in pigs, the people who work among them and pork products is an issue gaining momentum with groups favoring severe restrictions on the use of antibiotics in food animals.

The National Pork Board is trying to quell concerns while assuring the public that the issue is being taken seriously.

University of Minnesota researchers reported earlier this summer [2008] that they [had] found MRSA in 7.1% of 113 swine veterinarians tested.

Public health doctors at the University of Iowa found MRSA on nasal swabs from 147 of 209 pigs from one sow flow.

Ontario Veterinary College researcher Scott Weese last year [2007] detected such bacteria in 10% of 212 samples of ground pork and pork chops from four Canadian provinces.

"I think we can say it's likely that pork producers, as well as swine veterinarians, may have a higher carriage rate of MRSA in their nasal passages or skin," said Dr. Liz Wagstrom, assistant vice president of science and technology with the Pork Board. "What we don't see is any evidence that those people have any higher incidence of illness caused by MRSA than the general public. Just because they carry it in their skin or nose doesn't mean they're going to get sick or have serious consequences."

The Public Does Not Understand

That's a difficult concept for the general public to digest, according to Wagstrom.

"The general public doesn't seem to understand that carriage of something doesn't necessarily cause disease," she said. "It's very difficult for them to understand.

"The only way the average consumer might be able to get MRSA from pigs is if it was a foodborne illness,"

Wagstrom added. "We are confident that it's not. We also have no evidence that MRSA prevalence in pigs is tied in any way to use of antibiotics."

The House Agriculture Committee looked into the MRSA issue last winter and sought input from the Centers for Disease Control & Prevention (CDC).

In a letter to committee members, CDC Director Julie Louise Gerberding wrote, "CDC and others have investigated numerous outbreaks of community-associated MRSA infections in the U.S., and in none of these investigations has animal exposure been identified as a risk factor for infection."

Although pork producers and swine veterinarians may have a higher percentage of MRSA in their nasal passages and skin, this does not mean that they will have a higher rate of infections, compared with the general public. (© Panacea Pictures/ Alamy)

Lobbyists Use Scare Tactics

Groups such as Keep Antibiotics Working, the Union of Concerned Scientists and others are pushing legislation aimed at placing stiff restrictions on the use of antibiotics in food animals, and they use the public's increasing concern over MRSA-related illness in their lobbying and public communications efforts.

"This is a flash point activists try to use to say that we should stop using antibiotics, especially in animal feeds," Wagstrom said. "That doesn't really make any sense because we've never used methicillin in pork production. We're really unsure if antibiotic use in any way is a contributor."

Wagstrom cited a study conducted at an organic hog farm in another country where 100% of the animals tested positive for MRSA bacteria.

"Every animal they tested was positive," she said. "That would lead us to believe that antibiotics are not the only thing that could cause this, and they may not be involved at all."

At the [2008] American Veterinary Medical Assn. (AVMA) convention in New Orleans, La., a resolution was introduced in support of a ban on the use of growth-promoting antibiotics. While the resolution never made it to the full body for a vote, Wagstrom said the MRSA scare was prominent during committee discussions.

FAST FACT

A University of Maryland study found MRSA in only one out of three hundred pork samples from the Washington, DC, area.

"It's an attention-getting mechanism for that issue," she said. "Several consumer groups have really gotten after (the U.S. Department of Agriculture [USDA]) for not testing meats and (the Food & Drug Administration) for not conducting surveillance on MRSA as a potential foodborne agent. It's one more way to try to build consumer fear about the antibiotic issue and support their agenda to limit the use of antibiotics by agriculture."

Proactive Research

As food safety issues like the recent cases of *Salmonella*-related illness and outbreaks of *Escherichia coli* bacterial infections from ground beef become more prominent,

Congress is increasingly questioning whether the [government] is doing enough about foodborne illnesses.

USDA acknowledged that it isn't testing for MRSA—something an AVMA official said is understandable, according to a [2008] *Wall Street Journal* article.

"This is something we cannot ignore, but it's a resource issue," Lyle Vogel, assistant executive vice president of AVMA, said, according to the article. Compared with *E. coli* and *Salmonella* infections, "it does not seem to rise to the top of the priority list."

The Pork Board is currently funding research projects on the issue.

The University of Minnesota just recently started testing retail meats and continues to test pigs going to packing plants, in addition to the already completed study of swine veterinarians.

The University of Iowa, University of Minnesota and Ohio State University are cooperating on a study looking at the prevalence of MRSA in pigs and hog farm workers and comparing antibiotic-free herds with those that are more conventional in their antibiotic usage.

"We're still in fact-finding mode, but the industry is taking this seriously," said Wagstrom. "We're proactively out there conducting research and trying to assess any potential risk and get ahead of it to determine if there is a problem."

The Pork Board is also addressing the issue from an occupational health standpoint, according to Wagstrom.

"A research project will be looking at shower rooms and kitchen facilities at the barns to see if protocols can be developed that are used in gyms or other areas where they have a lot of traffic and human-to-human contact," she said. "I don't know that anybody's got any answers yet about whether this higher carriage rate is actually going to cause an increased number of illnesses. It doesn't appear to be as invasive as the bad strains of MRSA, but we just have to figure out if there's a worker or occupational safety concern, and if there is, how do we best protect our workers?"

Scientists Need to Investigate the Potential MRSA Threat from Bedbugs

US Senate Office of Sherrod Brown

The following excerpt of a press release from the office of US senator Sherrod Brown documents a formal request from the senator to the Centers for Disease Control and Prevention (CDC). In light of news about bedbugs in Vancouver, British Columbia, Canada, being infected with MRSA, Brown asks the CDC to investigate the public health implications of such a discovery and to develop a strategy if it turns out that bedbugs can transmit the bacteria to humans. Brown also plans to reintroduce into Congress the Strategies to Address Antimicrobial Resistance Act, which would strengthen federal efforts to address the growing problem of antibiotic resistance. The full text of Brown's letter is included in this selection.

After Vancouver [Canada]-based researchers discovered several instances of bed bugs infected with Methicillin-resistant *Staphylococcus aureus* (MRSA)

SOURCE: US Senate Office of Sherrod Brown, "Following Reports of Bed Bugs Infected with Potentially Fatal MRSA Bacteria, Brown Asks CDC to Investigate Public Health Implications," press release, May 13, 2011. www.brown.senate.gov. Courtesy of the Office of Senator Brown, Washington DC, 20510.

as well as vancomycin-resistant *Enterococcus faecium* (VRE), U.S. Sen. Sherrod Brown (D-OH) this week [May 12, 2011] asked the Centers for Disease Control and Prevention [CDC] to investigate the public health implications and develop an action plan to prevent a public health epidemic in the United States if bed bugs are in fact capable of transmitting disease to humans. Research conducted in Detroit, Michigan, also found MRSA in supermarket meat.

More Than a Nuisance?

There have been widespread reports in Ohio this year of bed bug infestations, with the City of Canton's environmental health director describing one local home as having the worst infestation he has ever seen.

"Until now, we thought bed bugs were simply a nuisance, not a means of transmitting disease," Brown said. "If, in fact, bed bugs can transmit MRSA and other harmful infections to humans, the CDC needs to outline an action plan immediately to help stem a health threat. Given the increasing prevalence of bed bug infestations in homes and public facilities alike, the American public needs assurance now that these bugs will not lead to a widespread outbreak of potentially fatal infections like MRSA." . . .

Brown's Letter to the CDC

May 12, 2011
Thomas R. Frieden, MD, MPH
Director
Centers for Disease Control and Prevention
1600 Clifton Road
Atlanta, Georgia 30333

Dear Director Frieden:

I am writing to urge you to review two new reports regarding methicillin-resistant *Staphylococcus aureus* (MRSA). A study conducted by Canadian scientists found MSRA in a small sample of bed bugs, while research conducted in Detroit, Michigan, found MRSA in supermarket meat. Both were published Wednesday [May 11, 2011] by your publication, *Emerging Infectious Diseases.*

MRSA infections can be acquired in community and medical settings and are exacerbated by antibiotic-resistant bacteria. As you are aware, antibiotics resistance is on the rise—creating more antibiotic-resistant pathogens. According to a recent study, more than 94,000 invasive MRSA infections occurred in the United States in 2005 and more than 18,500 of these infections resulted in death.

While bed bugs are currently a nuisance, they have not carried the same public health concerns associated with other pests, such as ticks or mosquitoes. Researchers in

Canadian researchers have discovered several instances of bedbugs infected with MRSA. (© Stephen Dalton/Photo Researchers, Inc.)

Vancouver, Canada recently found MRSA and vancomycin-resistant *Enterococcus faecium* (VRE) in bed bugs taken from patients at a Vancouver hospital. While little is known beyond the presence of MRSA in both the bed bugs and patients in question, if bed bugs are transmitting MRSA to humans, the Centers for Disease Control and Prevention (CDC) should outline an action plan to: 1) determine if bed bugs in the United States have MRSA in their systems; and 2) what can be done to prevent a public health epidemic.

Additionally, I am concerned that consumers are unknowingly exposing themselves to MRSA-tainted supermarket meat. While the CDC has already stated that bacteria can be killed by properly cooking meat and washing surfaces, I am concerned that this guidance does not reflect the serious dangers associated with MRSA infections.

Already this year, Ohio has experienced two MRSA outbreaks in one county alone. These infections are not only dangerous, but incredibly disruptive to the schools, hospitals, and workplaces at which they are contracted. This Congress, I plan to reintroduce the Strategies to Address Antimicrobial Resistance (STAAR) Act. The STAAR Act would strengthen federal antimicrobial resistance surveillance, prevention and control, and research efforts, as well as enhance the collection of critical information on the use of antibiotics in humans and animals.

However, prior to Congressional intervention, the CDC should develop a strategy to address potential MRSA transmission from bed bugs to humans. Prior to this discovery in Vancouver, concern over bed bugs was constrained to troublesome bites and infestations—not deadly infections. I urge the CDC to investigate whether bed bugs in the United States have MRSA and if they can

FAST FACT

Vancouver, BC; New York, NY; Washington, DC, and other cities have seen an alarming increase in bedbug infestations in recent years, due in part to the bugs' resistance to available pesticides.

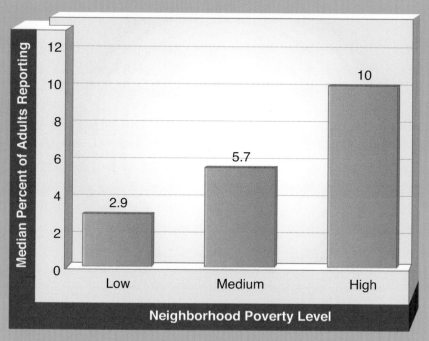

Adults Reporting Bedbugs in Their Homes, by Neighborhood Poverty Level, 2009

Median Percent of Adults Reporting

Low: 2.9
Medium: 5.7
High: 10

Neighborhood Poverty Level

Taken from: New York City Environmental Public Health and Sustainability Tracking Portal, New York City Community Health Survey, 2009.

transmit the infection to humans. Additionally, the CDC should consider drafting guidelines for handling and cooking meat in light of the discovery in Michigan.

I appreciate you taking the time to review my concerns. I look forward to your prompt response.

Sincerely,
Sherrod Brown
United States Senator

There Is No Evidence That Bedbugs Can Transmit MRSA

Marissa Cevallos

There is no proof that bedbugs can transmit the MRSA bacteria to humans, notes Marissa Cevallos in the following viewpoint. As entomology researchers at Purdue University explain, bedbugs have been known to carry some viruses, bacteria, and parasites, but no evidence has been found that these disease agents can survive for long inside a bedbug or that they can be spread by the bite of a bedbug. While it is possible that scratching a bedbug bite can leave the skin vulnerable to MRSA infection, the threat of catching MRSA from a bedbug bite is only theoretical, the author concludes. Cevallos is a health writer for the *Los Angeles Times*.

Not only can bedbugs harbor MRSA, they could potentially, just maybe, spread the drug-resistant bacteria, researchers—and resulting headlines—are speculating. The thought is a scary one, but not much different than what we already knew about the threat from these generally nocturnal parasites.

Bedbugs and Disease Transmission

It's certainly plausible that a blood-sucking bug can spread blood-transmitted diseases, but scientists haven't found much evidence they do so. Here's the low-down on what's known on bedbugs and disease.

The Entomology Department at Purdue University says this: "At least 27 agents of human disease have been found in bed bugs, including viruses, bacteria, protozoa, and parasitic worms. None of these agents reproduce or

Bedbug bites on a patient's back are shown here. Twenty-seven agents of human disease have been found in bed-bugs, but some experts say there is no evidence that they directly transmit diseases to humans. (© SPL/Photo Researchers, Inc.)

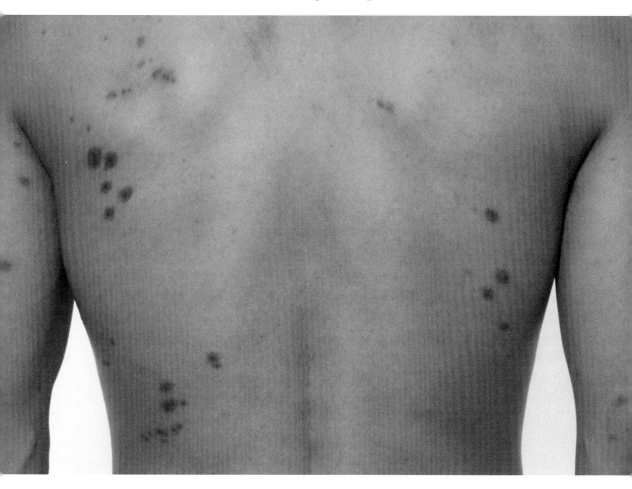

multiply within bed bugs, and very few survive for any length of time inside a bed bug. There is no evidence that bed bugs are involved in the transmission (via bite or infected feces) of any disease agent, including hepatitis B virus and HIV, the virus that causes AIDS."

Again, there's that "no evidence" of disease transmission —just the plausibility. A report in the Centers for Disease Control and Prevention journal *Emerging Infectious Diseases* in 2005 has this to say about bedbugs and disease transmission:

> Although bed bugs could theoretically act as a disease vector, as is the case with body lice, which transmit *Bartonella quintana* (the causal agent of trench fever) among homeless persons, bed bugs have never been shown to transmit disease in vivo [within a living organism]. Hepatitis B viral DNA can be detected in bed bugs up to 6 weeks after they feed on infectious blood, but no transmission of hepatitis B infection was found in a chimpanzee model. Transmission of hepatitis C is unlikely, since hepatitis C viral RNA is not detectable in bed bugs after an infectious blood meal. Live HIV can be recovered from bed bugs up to 1 hour after they feed on infected blood, but no epidemiologic evidence for HIV transmission by this route exists.

FAST FACT

According to the Centers for Disease Control and Prevention, the research study that discovered bedbugs carrying MRSA did not determine whether the bacteria were on the exterior of each bug or living inside the bug.

An article from Medscape echoes that HIV spread is unlikely but that anaphylaxis, a severe allergic reaction, has been documented. And the article raises the possibility of itchy ("pruritic") bug bites becoming infected: "Sometimes, if the bite reactions are intensely pruritic, scratching with excoriations may be complicated by impetigo." Impetigo is a skin infection caused by strep or staph bacteria—and that includes MRSA, according to PubMed Health. That's the hypothetical situation—

The Life Cycle of the Bedbug

Female bedbugs lay about five eggs (1) daily throughout their adult lives in a sheltered location (mattress seams, crevices in box springs, spaces under baseboards, etc). The bugs will undergo five nymphal stages (2, 3, 4, 5, 6), each one requiring a blood meal before molting to the next stage, with the fifth stage molting into an adult (7). Nymphs and adults take about 5–10 minutes to obtain a full blood meal. Adults live 6–12 months and may survive for long periods of time without feeding.

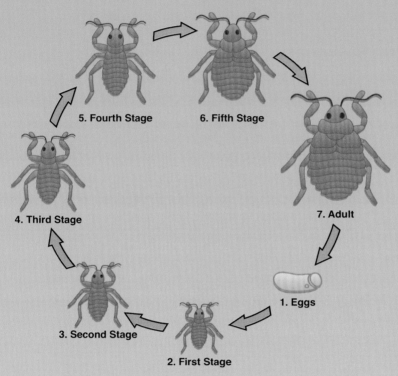

5. Fourth Stage

6. Fifth Stage

4. Third Stage

7. Adult

1. Eggs

3. Second Stage

2. First Stage

Taken from: DPDx, "Parasites and Health: Bed Bugs," Centers for Disease Control and Prevention, October 27, 2011. ww.dpd.cdc.gov/dpdx/html/Bedbugs.htm.

scratching a bug bite that leaves the skin vulnerable to infection by MRSA—researchers suggested this week [May 12, 2011]. That's not to say researchers aren't still working on trying to quantify the potential threat of bedbugs. A clinical trial is under way in France. But again, the threat remains largely theoretical. Interesting, but theoretical.

MRSA Spreads Quickly Through Homosexual Activity

Matthew Cullinan Hoffman

In the following selection, Matthew Cullinan Hoffman reports on a study appearing in the *Annals of American Medicine* that concludes that a virulent form of MRSA is spreading through homosexual activity. The study suggests that there is a link between a flesh-eating strain of MRSA and certain high-risk behaviors, such as anal sex, sex with multiple partners, and the use of illicit drugs. In San Francisco, an area with a high population of homosexuals, gay men are thirteen times more likely to be infected with MRSA, the author points out. Hoffman writes for LifeSiteNews.com, a nonprofit Internet service dedicated to issues of life, culture, and family.

A new medical study appearing in the *Annals of American Medicine* shows that homosexuals are spreading a new, highly-infectious flesh-eating bacteria amongst themselves, most probably through anal intercourse. The bacterium, called MRSA USA300, is impervious to front-line antibiotics and can only be treated with rarer drugs, primarily vancomycin. Researchers say that the bug, which is a type of *Staphylococcus*, is primed to develop immunity to that drug as well. Infected patients may have inflammation, abscesses, and tissue loss in the affected areas. Although the bacterium does not literally "eat" the body, it manufactures toxins that can cause "necrosis"—the death of surrounding tissue.

Unhealthy Behavior Is the Driving Force

The study's authors note that the strong link between unhealthy behavior, particularly among homosexuals, is the driving force behind the disease. "Spread of the USA300 clone among men who have sex with men is associated with high-risk behaviors, including use of methamphetamine and other illicit drugs, sex with multiple partners,

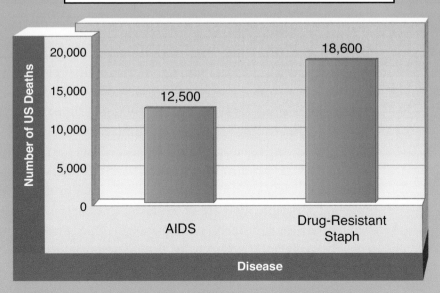

**AIDS Versus MRSA
Number of US Deaths, 2005***

*AIDS figures are preliminary; staph figures are estimated.

Taken from: American Medical Association.

participation in a group sex party, use of the internet for sexual contacts, skin-abrading sex, and history of sexually transmitted infections," the authors write.

"The same patterns of increased sexual risk behaviors among men who have sex with men—which have resulted from changes in beliefs regarding HIV disease severity with the availability of potent antiretroviral therapy— have been driving resurgent epidemics of early syphilis, rectal gonorrhea, and new HIV infections in San Francisco, Boston, and elsewhere," add the researchers.

The study, which focused on clinics in the San Francisco area, found that in some cases up to 39% of patients had the MRSA USA300 infections in their genitals or buttocks, although the disease can be spread by general skin-to-skin contact and can even be picked up from surfaces. Observing that "infection with multidrug-resistant USA300 MRSA is common among men who have sex with men," the study timidly concludes that "multidrug-resistant MRSA infection might be sexually transmitted in this population," and counsels "further research."

> ## FAST FACT
>
> Twelve percent of MRSA infections are now community associated, according to the *New York Times*.

Another Homosexual Epidemic

It is estimated that in San Francisco's Castro District, which has the highest concentration of homosexuals in the country, the infection rate is 1 in every 588 residents. One in every 3,800 residents of San Francisco are infected. Homosexuals are 13 times more likely to be infected than others in the city.

The disease is not only spreading in San Francisco, but also Boston, New York and Los Angeles. In addition to homosexuals, people who are ill or have weakened immune systems are particularly susceptible. MRSA and other types of *Staphylococcus* bacteria, often spread in hospitals, kill more than 19,000 Americans each year, a rate higher than deaths due to AIDS.

Peter LaBarbara, president of Americans for Truth About Homosexuality, is hoping that the revelation of yet another homosexual epidemic will have an impact on the public's perception of homosexual behavior. "I think that the media, and Hollywood, and a lot of our policy makers and certainly academia are in a world of 'let's pretend' with regard to homosexual behavior and its consequences," he told LifeSiteNews. "They don't want to focus on the special risks that homosexual behavior, especially between men, have in the public health arena, and issues like this keep coming up." However, LaBarbara acknowledges that the major media will "invariably spin things in a homosexual direction."

San Francisco's Castro District has the highest concentration of gays in America. The MRSA infection rate for homosexuals is reportedly thirteen times higher than for heterosexuals. (**AP Images/ Darryl Bush**)

"We saw the identical thing happen 25 years ago with the reporting on AIDS," he said, "but ironically the whole AIDS crisis strengthened the homosexual lobby in this country."

Homosexual Activity Is Not a Primary Cause of the Spread of MRSA

Tim Murphy

In 2008 research studies about the MRSA virus spreading among gay men were poorly worded and misleading, argues Tim Murphy in the following selection. The studies became the subject of a homophobic media frenzy, with tabloids and right-wing groups claiming that gay men could spread deadly infections to the general population. The truth is that MRSA can be transmitted by any kind of direct physical contact, regardless of whether that contact is of a sexual nature, Murphy explains. In addition, most of the men who participated in the 2008 studies were HIV positive, so it is possible that the higher rate of MRSA among these men was due to their having compromised immune systems. Murphy is a writer in New York City who has contributed to the *New York Times*, the *Advocate*, *Out*, and *Poz*.

In mid January [2008] researchers in San Francisco and Boston sparked a global press circus when they reported that a virulent, multidrug-resistant form of staph bacteria (specifically, methicillin-resistant *Staphylococcus aureus*, or MRSA) was spreading among gay men. According to the report, Bay Area gays were 13 times more likely to be infected than area residents in general. Epidemiologist Binh An Diep, the lead researcher, summed up the findings this way: "Once this reaches the general population, it will be truly unstoppable."

The world press went wild. A London tabloid called the bug "the new HIV." An Australian paper ran the headline "Flesh-Eating Bug Spreads Among Gays." Right-wing groups piled on: "Gays May Spread Deadly Staph Infection to General Population," blared a missive from Concerned Women for America.

Homophobic Hysteria

The hysteria echoed homophobic headlines from the early days of AIDS, and gay newspapers and activists quickly struck back, pointing out that MRSA was already widely reported in "the general population" and wasn't transmitted primarily through sex. "I've lost count of how many times I've seen this depressing drill about gay men, our sexuality, diseases, and researchers generating great headlines for their academic careers," wrote activist Michael Petrelis on his blog.

Within days the University of California, San Francisco, researchers apologized. In their revised press release they down-played the role of gay men and removed the hot-button medical term "general population." Researcher Henry Chambers told *The Advocate* [magazine] that Diep was a rookie researcher who "was not thinking about the consequences" of his word choices. "He meant that [MRSA] is more prevalent in the gay population," said Chambers, "and that it might become as prevalent in other populations as well."

The Facts

Now that the kerfuffle is behind us, let's get to the facts. MRSA is not spread just through sex. It appears most commonly in hospital settings and among groups, such as football players or wrestlers, engaging in frequent skin-to-skin contact or contact with shared mats, clothes, towels, razors, and the like. It didn't originate among gays, but doctors who treat gay men in New York City, Boston, San Francisco, and Chicago say that since 2000 they have seen a marked increase in MRSA, which is resistant to penicillin antibiotics but treatable with other drugs. As for the scary "flesh-eating" moniker, in rare cases, MRSA—which begins with

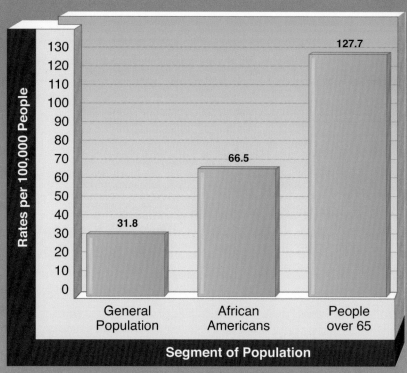

Rates of Invasive MRSA in the United States

Taken from: Dennis O'Brien, "Superbug Defies Antibiotics," *Baltimore Sun*, March 1, 2008.

what usually resembles a pimple or a spider bite and blows up painfully over a few days into a pus-filled abscess—can damage skin tissue. But again, that's rare.

Ken Mayer, medical research director of Boston's LGBT [lesbian, gay, bisexual, and transgender]-serving Fenway Community Health (which reported the Boston end of the study), says that Fenway currently sees one to two cases of MRSA a week. It's a clear increase over the past few years but not an epidemic. Tom Barrett, chief medical officer of Chicago's LGBT-focused Howard Brown Health Center, says, "Now when we see a skin infection we assume it's MRSA, because every [skin infection] we've cultured [in the lab] for several months is."

Because sex involves skin-to-skin contact, MRSA can be spread that way, which is likely why many gay men get the infection in their genital area. Of particular concern are users of drugs like crystal meth, because hours of drug-fueled sex can abrade the skin and let the infection in, especially if participants go a long time without showering. But people can also pick up infections at the gym (wear flip-flops in the showers!) and other random places. "Most of the time," says Barrett, "we haven't traced cases to sexual encounters."

MRSA and HIV

Is MRSA the new HIV? Not quite. HIV is hard to transmit sexually outside of anal and vaginal intercourse, whereas MRSA can be transmitted through naked frottage [rubbing] alone. (Transmission through kissing or a handshake is unlikely.) Numerous studies find MRSA more common among HIV-positive gay men than their HIV-negative counterparts—in fact, the controversial report initially obscured the fact that all the cases reviewed in San

> **FAST FACT**
>
> In 2008 the Centers for Disease Control and Prevention released a statement reporting that MRSA infections "occur in men, women, adults, children, and persons of all races and sexual orientations."

Francisco and about half from Boston were in HIV-positive men—but it's unclear whether that's because the immune systems of HIV-positive men are more vulnerable or because many choose to have sex only with other HIV-positive men, thereby spreading MRSA among that group.

Yes, gay men have registered a recent rise in both MRSA and HIV (the Centers for Disease Control and Prevention tracked a 13% increase in HIV among gay men between 2001 and 2005). But "they're parallel phenomena," says Ken Mayer. "I don't think one is causing the other."

The MRSA takeaway? Pretty simple: To prevent it, wash your hands often with antibacterial soap and shower after any skin-to-skin contact or contact with possibly infected surfaces. Don't share towels, clothes, or other personal supplies with people with staph. And clean and cover any cuts or wounds.

Treating Staph Infections

If you have what looks like a spider bite or pimple, don't try to pop it, and if it starts leaking pus, cover it. If it grows rather than fades over a few days, get to a doctor. Now that MRSA is a known villain in the world at large, most doctors should be on the lookout for it, but just in case, suggest to your doctor that it be cultured to determine the best antibiotic.

Treatment typically involves lancing and draining the abscess, which will often do the trick, says Gal Mayer, medical director of New York City's LGBT-serving Callen-Lorde Community Health Center. But these days many doctors will assume it's MRSA and start patients right away on nonpenicillin drugs like Bactrim, clindamycin, or tetracycline. (The San Francisco–Boston study reported on a newer strain of MRSA that's resistant to two of those three meds.) In some cases hospitalization for IV [intravenous] treatment is required, as vividly demonstrated

To prevent MRSA infection, wash the hands with soap and water after touching surfaces that could be infected and shower after skin-to-skin contact.
(© Jeffrey Blackler/ Alamy)

when Project Runway contestant Jack Mackenroth left the competition in an episode aired in December [2007] for an infection in his nose.

The bottom line is that MRSA isn't just about sex and it isn't limited to gays, but you still have to be careful. Just ask Ryan Rivera, 42, a New York City fund-raising executive who says that he and his boyfriend are both HIV-negative and monogamous. Rivera got MRSA in the summer of 2005 when he and his partner were renovating their apartment, wearing shorts and kicking up "lots of dust and dirt and germs and mold." He was hospitalized for four days and took Bactrim for a few weeks. The recent coverage "twisting it into the whole gay infection thing" infuriated him: "I've done enough research to know that it didn't start with gay guys, and it's not going to end with gay guys."

Hospitals Should Screen Patients for MRSA

Meg Haskell

In the following selection, Meg Haskell discusses pending legislation in Maine that would require hospitals in the state to screen patients at high risk for MRSA before admitting them. High-risk patients include those who have recently been released from another hospital, nursing home, or correctional facility; patients with open wounds; patients being admitted to intensive care; and patients undergoing dialysis, joint replacement, or heart surgery. If any of these patients are carrying MRSA, they would be kept in a private room or with another MRSA-carrying patient, the bill stipulates. The legislation would also require hospitals to report MRSA data to the Centers for Disease Control and Prevention and make the information publicly available, Haskell points out. Supporters contend that passing this law would reduce the incidence of MRSA in Maine hospitals. Haskell is the health editor for the *Bangor Daily News*.

SOURCE: Meg Haskell, "Bill Seeks to Reduce MRSA and Other Hospital-Acquired Infections," *Bangor (ME) Daily News*, February 5, 2011. http://bangordailynews.com. Copyright © 2011 by Bangor Daily News. All rights reserved. Reproduced by permission.

P olitical tides may ebb and flow, but for victims of hospital-acquired methicillin resistant *Staphylococcus aureus*, or MRSA, the opportunity is always at hand to improve patient safety. New legislation is pending in Augusta [Maine's capital] to strengthen recent MRSA tracking, prevention and reporting, not only in Maine hospitals but in nursing homes as well. Support for the effort crosses partisan lines, but pits cost-conscious hospitals against consumers and others in the health care community.

MRSA has brought disability and fear into the life of 62-year-old Norm Pacholski of Hermon. In September of last year [2010], months after undergoing a knee replacement for longstanding injuries suffered while serving in the U.S. Army, Pacholski experienced a sudden, severe pain and inflammation in the new knee. Testing of fluid pulled from the infected knee confirmed the presence of MRSA. Repeated hospitalizations and surgeries have left him unable to work, drive or bear weight on his right leg, and dependent on his wife Coco for many activities he once undertook easily on his own. He's scheduled later this month [February 2011] for another try at a new titanium knee, hoping this time to avoid complications. "This can happen to anyone," he said. "You go into a hospital, you don't know what you're going to come out with."

A Bill to Protect High-Risk Patients

The MRSA bacteria commonly is present on the skin and in the nasal passages of healthy people and often causes no illness. But especially in patients with weakened immune systems, it can infect the urinary tract, the blood, the lungs, open wounds and other body sites. Because it is resistant to most antibiotics, it can be lethal as well as lead to amputations and organ failure. It often is acquired in institutional settings such as nursing homes and hospitals, where it may be easily passed from one vulnerable

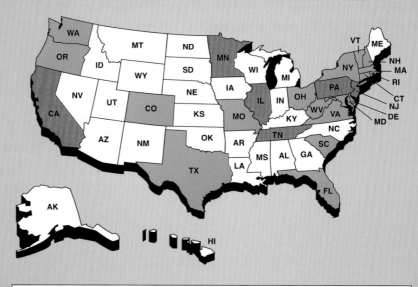

State Laws Relating to Hospital Acquired Infections

Public reporting laws

Public reporting laws and infection prevention laws

Taken from: Centers for Disease Control and Prevention/Allnurses.com, August 2, 2009.
www.cdc.gov and http://allnurses.com.

patient to another, often by nurses, doctors and other staff, as well as by visitors who do not practice careful hand washing and other infection control strategies.

A bill submitted by Rep. Adam Goode, D-Bangor, would require all Maine hospitals to screen high-risk patients for MRSA prior to admitting them, beginning Jan. 1, 2012. As defined in the bill, high-risk patients include those who:

- Are admitted from another hospital or nursing facility or who have been discharged from a hospital or nursing facility within one year.
- Are admitted from a correctional facility.

- Are admitted to the hospital intensive care unit.
- Receive renal dialysis for kidney failure.
- Have open lesions that appear to be infected.
- Are admitted for joint replacement or cardiac surgery.

The bill also would require nursing homes to screen all patients for MRSA upon admission. The screening process consists of using a sterile swab to collect a sample from the inside of the nose. Patients found to be carrying MRSA would have to be housed in a private room or with another MRSA-carrying patient. Visitors and staff would be required to observe contact precautions including gloves, gowns and masks. In addition to MRSA testing and management, the bill would require hospitals to report MRSA data to the National Health Safety Network at the U.S. Centers for Disease Control and Prevention and to make the information publicly available upon request. Information on the prevalence of other drug-resistant organisms, such as *Clostridium difficile*, would also be collected and made public. Goode says the bill is intended to encourage hospitals to improve their infection control practices while at the same time helping health care consumers select high-performing institutions for themselves and their loved ones. "My general feeling is that there is a fair way to compare rates of MRSA among the hospitals in Maine and that the information should be publicly accessible for patients trying to choose a hospital to care for them," Goode said.

> **FAST FACT**
>
> According to bacteriologist Frank DeLeo, staph is the number one cause of heart and soft-tissue infections.

Jeff Austin, spokesman for the Maine Hospital Association, said the organization is still reviewing Goode's bill but likely will oppose it. Hospitals should report actual patient infection rates, he said, but in requiring screening of certain patient populations and insisting on isolation and precautions for patients who are not symptomatic,

Goode's bill oversteps its regulatory intent and seeks to legislate actual patient care.

A similar bill in 2009, also sponsored by Goode, led to a requirement for all Maine hospitals to screen high-risk patients for six months and report results to the Maine Quality Forum office of the quasi-state Dirigo Health Agency. The results of that project, which wrapped up in June 2010, are still being compiled into a formal report which will be shared with the Legislature's Health and Human Services Committee. Ellen Schneiter, who recently took over as director of the Maine Quality Forum, said the value of the report is limited by differences in the way hospitals interpreted and reported the screening data.

Hospitals Can Eliminate MRSA

Goode's bill was drafted with support from Bangor resident Kathy Day, a retired nurse whose father died after contracting MRSA infection in his lungs following a routine admission to a small rural hospital in northern Maine. Day says her father's untimely death raised her awareness about the prevalence and severity of MRSA infections. "I learned it is preventable. There are hospitals

Maine state representative Adam Goode (standing) introduced a bill that would require all Maine hospitals to screen high-risk patients for MRSA prior to admitting them. (© AP Images/Robert F. Bukaty)

that have succeeded in reducing and even eliminating MRSA," she said. "Maine hospitals aren't doing that." Day referenced a 2001 MRSA reduction pilot program at the VA [Veterans Administration] Pittsburgh Healthcare System that was expanded in 2007 to more than 150 VA hospitals throughout the nation. The effort incorporates universal MRSA screening and isolation of patients.

Day said passage of Goode's bill, LD 267, is essential to reducing the incidence of MRSA and other health care associated infections in Maine's hospitals, nursing homes and communities. "Unless somebody has a family member or a loved one who has suffered from this, they just don't know the impact," she said. By pressuring institutions to appropriately identify, isolate and treat patients harboring drug-resistant organisms, Day said, tragedies like her father's death and Norm Pacholski's long struggle to regain his health and independence can be avoided.

Hospital Screening Does Not Reduce MRSA Infections

Dennis O'Brien

Researchers in Switzerland have found that prescreening incoming hospital patients for MRSA has no effect on the rate of MRSA infections in hospitals, reports Dennis O'Brien in the following article. Moreover, the Maryland state senate decided against legislation that would have required such hospital screenings. Opponents of the legislation, as well as the Maryland Hospital Association, maintain that safeguards against MRSA are evolving and that there is no reason to have legally entrenched guidelines. O'Brien is a reporter for the *Baltimore Sun*, a daily newspaper.

Less than a month after the Maryland General Assembly rejected a bill that would have required hospitals to test incoming patients for the dangerous MRSA bacterium, researchers in Switzerland are reporting that screening doesn't reduce MRSA infections. Re-

SOURCE: Dennis O'Brien, "Screening Not Found to Limit MRSA: Wards That Test for 'Superbug' No Better Off than Nontesters," *Baltimore (MD) Sun*, March 12, 2008. http://articles.baltimoresun .com. Copyright © 2008 by The Baltimore Sun. All rights reserved. Reproduced by permission.

searchers found that MRSA infection rates in wards where patients were pre-screened for the superbug were no different from infection rates in areas without screening, according to an article in today's [March 12, 2008] *Journal of the American Medical Association.* "It's just not very helpful," said Dr. Stephan Harbarth, the epidemiologist who led the study at the University of Geneva Hospitals.

The Swiss Study

Harbarth examined MRSA infection rates among 21,754 patients treated in 12 surgical wards. His researchers tested incoming patients in half the wards for nine months and then switched testing to the other half for nine months. Screening on admission identified 515 patients with MRSA—including 337 who would have otherwise been missed, according to the study. Infected patients were isolated, treated by personnel wearing gowns and gloves, cleaned with antimicrobials and given medications adjusted for the infection.

A nurse prepares a nasal swab to test a patient for MRSA. Researchers in Switzerland have found that prescreening incoming hospital patients for MRSA has had no effect on MRSA infection rates in hospitals. (© **Danny Lawson/PA Photos**/Landov)

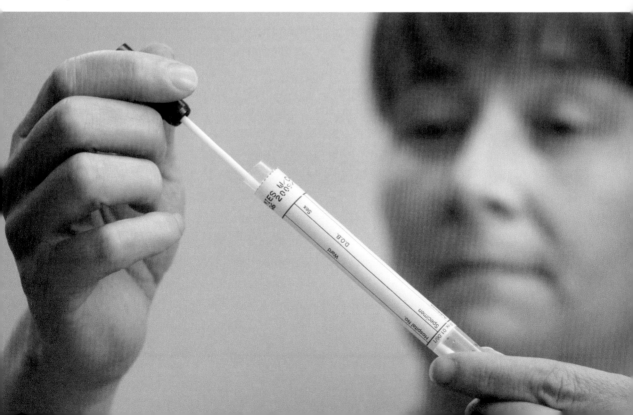

But the researchers found that only 93 additional patients developed MRSA while in wards where screening was conducted, compared with 76 in nonscreened wards—a difference they consider insignificant. "There was not even the slightest trend toward reduction of MRSA infections in the screening wards," Harbarth said. Harbarth recommends screening only in areas where the risk is highest: intensive care, critical care and cardiovascular surgical units. Critics said the duration and scope of the study were too limited. Because patients in some wards weren't screened, MRSA could survive to be spread by hospital personnel, they said.

A Deadly Superbug

MRSA, or Methicillin-resistant *Staphylococcus aureus*, is a bacterium that can live harmlessly in the skin or nose but will attack wounds and cause life-threatening infections, including pneumonia and blood poisoning, when someone is hospitalized. Over the years, it has evolved into a superbug that resists most common antibiotics.

> **FAST FACT**
>
> The journal *Clinical Infectious Diseases* reports that 4.5 million children up to the age of five are hospitalized each year for severe infections.

The federal Centers for Disease Control and Prevention estimates that MRSA caused 18,000 deaths in 2005. Last June [2007] a study by the Association for Professionals in Infection Control and Epidemiology (APIC) found MRSA in 46 out of every 1,000 hospital patients. The CDC also has identified at least 12 MRSA subtypes. One new variant at large in the population killed a Virginia youth last fall and can spread in gyms, locker rooms and other community settings.

Should Prescreening Be the Law?

State Sen. Lisa A. Gladden, a Baltimore Democrat, proposed legislation this year that would have required Maryland's hospitals to screen patients they consider at high

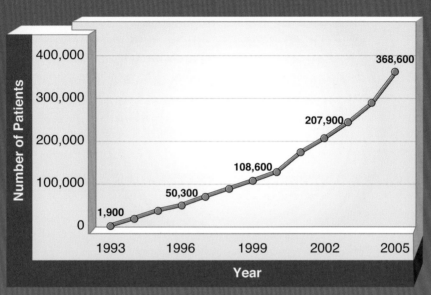

US Hospital Stays with MRSA Infections

Number of Patients

400,000

300,000

368,600

200,000

207,900

108,600

100,000

50,300

1,900

0

1993   1996   1999   2002   2005

Year

Taken from: Agency for Healthcare Research and Quality. "Hospital Stays with MRSA Infections 1993–2005," and Sally Church, "New Drug in Development May Destroy MRSA," May 21, 2008. www.eacademy.com.

risk of infection—such as those previously infected or transferred from nursing homes. Several states have enacted similar mandates, and the Department of Veterans Affairs recently began requiring its hospitals to conduct MRSA screenings.

But Gladden's legislation was killed in the Senate Finance Committee last month [February 2008] after the Maryland Hospital Association—along with a variety of health officials—argued that safeguards are evolving. The association is sponsoring public forums on MRSA at hospitals around the state.

The legislation's opponents said that the Swiss study supports their arguments that mandatory screening is unwise. "It reinforces my belief that embedding guidelines into law is just bad law," said Dr. William Minogue, executive director of the Maryland Patient Safety Center. "MRSA is a moving target."

But advocates for improved screening argue that the MRSA legislation is necessary because hospitals are moving too slowly in screening patients. "This does not invalidate the 200 studies that support the approach we've been advocating," said Michael Bennett, who as president of the Coalition for Patients Rights has fought unsuccessfully for MRSA legislation for three years. "Those who are against this are against this because they just don't want to be bothered with it."

Hand Sanitizers Are Not Proven to Prevent MRSA Infections

US Food and Drug Administration

In the following selection, the US Food and Drug Administration (FDA) warns consumers to avoid buying hand sanitizers and other antiseptic products that claim to prevent MRSA infections. These claims are unproven, and consumers are being misled if they believe that products from a drugstore can protect them from potentially dangerous infections. Companies that make such claims are breaking the law, the FDA points out. The best way to reduce the spread of infection is to frequently wash one's hands with soap and warm water. The FDA is responsible for protecting the public health by assuring the safety, efficacy, and security of drugs, biological products, medical devices, cosmetics, and food.

Some hand sanitizers and antiseptic products come with claims that they can prevent MRSA infections. Don't believe them. These statements are unproven, says the Food and Drug Administration (FDA). MRSA

SOURCE: Food and Drug Administration, "Hand Sanitizers Carry Unproven Claims to Prevent MRSA Infections," April 20, 2011. www.fda.gov.

(methicillin-resistant *Staphylococcus aureus*) is a bacterium that can cause severe—even life-threatening—infections that do not respond to standard treatment with the antibiotic methicillin.

An Aggressive Organism

"*Staphylococcus aureus* itself is a very aggressive organism," says Edward Cox, M.D., M.P.H., director of FDA's Office of Antimicrobial Products. "It's often associated with patients in hospitals who have weakened immune systems, but the bacterium can also cause significant skin infections and abscesses in a normal, healthy person. And it can get into the bloodstream and, less frequently, may involve the heart valve, which is very difficult to treat."

But this antibiotic-resistant strain is even more difficult to treat. "With MRSA, a number of the antibiotic drugs we typically use often don't work, so we lose treatment options we used to rely upon," says Cox.

Buyer Beware

FDA is cracking down on companies that break federal law by promoting their products as preventing MRSA infections and other diseases without agency review and approval. "Consumers are being misled if they think these products you can buy in a drug store or from other places will protect them from a potentially deadly infection," says Deborah Autor, compliance director at FDA's Center for Drug Evaluation and Research. FDA wants consumers to watch out for unproven product claims, too—whether they buy a product from a retail store or through the Internet. Examples of unproven claims found on product labels are:

- kills over 99.9% of MRSA
- helps prevent skin infections caused by MRSA and other germs
- is effective against a broad spectrum of pathogens, including MRSA

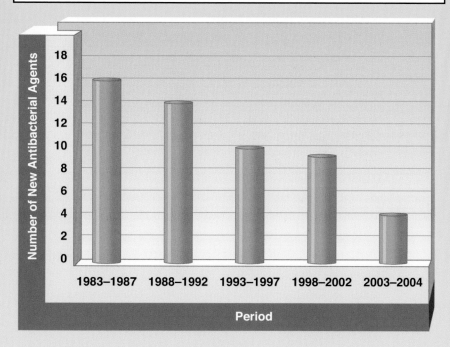

Number of New Antibacterial Agents Approved in the United States, 1983–2004

Number of New Antibacterial Agents

18
16
14
12
10
8
6
4
2
0

1983–1987   1988–1992   1993–1997   1998–2002   2003–2004

Period

Taken from: North American Center for Continuing Medical Education.

One company claims that its hand sanitizing lotion prevents infection from the bacterium *E. coli* and the H1N1 flu virus. And another firm claims its "patented formulation of essential plant oils" kills the bacterium *Salmonella*. These claims are also unproven and, therefore, illegal. "FDA has not approved any products claiming to prevent infection from MRSA, *E. coli, Salmonella,* or H1N1 flu, which a consumer can just walk into a store and buy," says Autor. "These products give consumers a false sense of protection."

FDA Warns Companies

On April 20, 2011, FDA issued Warning Letters to four companies that make or distribute the following products that can be bought over-the-counter (without a prescription):

- Staphaseptic First Aid Antiseptic/Pain Relieving Gel, by Tec Laboratories
- Safe4Hours Hand Sanitizing Lotion and Safe4Hours First Aid Antiseptic Skin Protectant, by JD Nelson and Associates
- Dr. Tichenor's Antiseptic Gel, by Dr. G.H. Tichenor Antiseptic Co.
- Clean Well All-Natural Hand Sanitizer, Clean Well All-Natural Hand Sanitizing Wipes, and Clean Well

The US Food and Drug Administration warns the public that hand sanitizers do not protect against MRSA, despite advertisers' claims to the contrary. (© Ronnie McMillan/ Alamy Images)

> All-Natural Antibacterial Foaming Hand Soap, by Oh So Clean Inc., also known as CleanWell Company

If the companies do not correct the violations explained in the Warning Letters within 15 days, FDA may seize the products or take other legal action.

Advice for Consumers

- Don't buy over-the-counter hand sanitizers or other products that claim to prevent infection from MRSA, *E. coli, Salmonella,* flu, or other bacteria or viruses.
- Ask your pharmacist or other health care professional for help in distinguishing between reliable and questionable information on product labels and company websites.
- In general, wash hands often, especially before handling food, to help avoid getting sick. Wash hands with warm water and soap for 20 seconds. For children, this means the time it takes to "sing the "Happy Birthday" song twice.
- If you find products on the Internet that you believe make false or unproven claims, tell FDA. . . .
- Report side effects that you think may be related to using hand sanitizers or other medical products to FDA's MedWatch Adverse Event Reporting Program either online, by regular mail, by fax, or by phone.

CHAPTER 3

Personal Experiences with MRSA

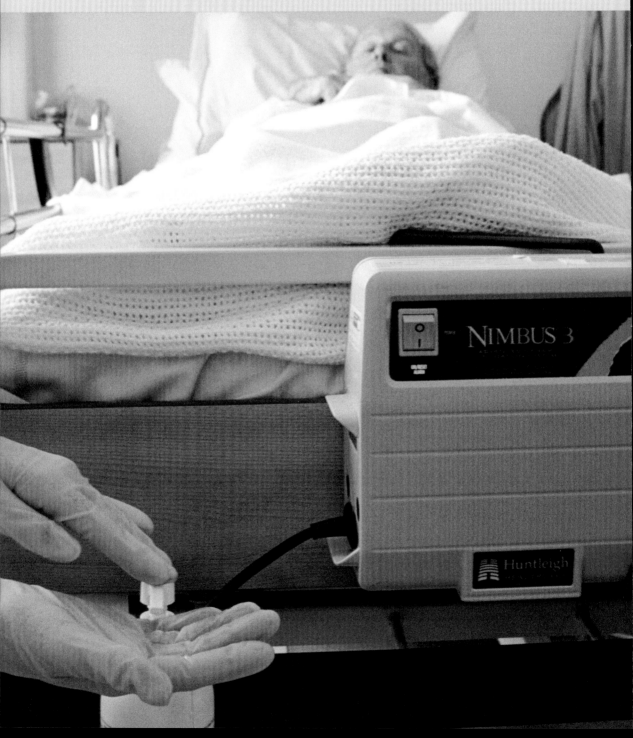

Facing Leg Amputation Because of MRSA

Judith Izenstain

Judith Izenstain, a resident of London, England, had to have surgery on her leg after breaking it in a fall. The day before she was to be discharged from the hospital, she became so weak that she was unable to sit up. A postoperative MRSA infection had apparently led to septicemia, pneumonia, and a collapsed lung. Izenstain believes she may have caught MRSA after a nurse changed her intravenous bag without taking proper sanitary precautions. Years after her initial operation, MRSA bacteria remain in her bone, and doctors may eventually have to amputate her leg.

When I went to hospital in June 2003 I was told I'd be in and out in a week—I'd only broken my left leg in a fall. The operation to put a plate in went well but at 4pm on the day before I was due to be discharged I began to feel weak and couldn't sit up. I have no recollection of the next 10 days until I woke up in isolation.

SOURCE: Judith Izenstain, "Your Life: I've Been Told I Need to Have My Leg Amputated," *Mirror*, January 18, 2009, p. 39. Copyright © 2009 by Mirrorpix. All rights reserved. Reproduced by permission.

Photo on facing page. A health care worker washes her hands. The spread of infections, including MRSA, can be curtailed by health workers simply washing their hands before and after every patient encounter.
(© **Mark Thomas/Photo Researchers, Inc.**)

When I came round, doctors didn't know if I would live or die. I had MRSA, which had triggered septicaemia, a collapsed lung and pneumonia.

Like Something from a Horror Film

When the doctors took the plaster off my leg two weeks later my skin was black and rotting and looked like something from a horror film. The stench was terrible. I was in shock. I couldn't believe it was happening to me. My recovery was slow and it took me months even to walk on crutches. I was discharged after three months, in September. By then, it appeared the MRSA had cleared but my leg was still weak.

I went from 10st [stone, a unit of weight equal to 14 pounds] 7lbs to less than 6st 7lbs and looked like an old woman. I live alone so it was hard. Luckily, friends popped round and did shopping, and the nurse came every other day.

Infection from a Needle

I now think I caught MRSA from a needle. A nurse wasn't wearing gloves when he opened the packet—and let it touch the bedclothes—when he changed the drip on my arm. Hours later, the area by the needle was sore. I'm convinced that's how MRSA got into my blood.

FAST FACT

MRSA is almost always spread by physical contact, not through the air.

I now have no quality of life. My leg has never healed properly. I can't walk unaided, I can't drive and I'm housebound. To make matters worse, the MRSA came back in January 2006—it had been dormant in my bone. I was rushed to hospital and, within days, my leg was five times its normal size. I was in agony. For the second time, doctors thought I was going to die. But I pulled through and the MRSA appeared to go away. I then had an operation to remove the infected knee bone.

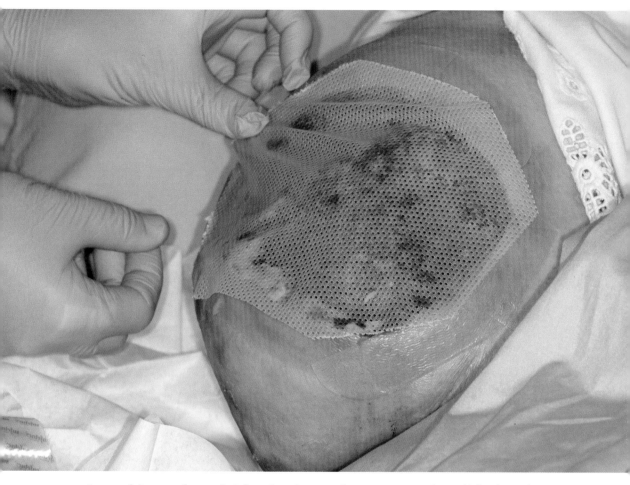

Later this year [2008], I face having my leg amputated. It hasn't healed and I'm in constant pain. I can't walk on it so there's no other solution and, apparently, the MRSA could still be dormant in my bone. My life is ruined but I try to stay positive. Other people have caught superbugs and died. At least I'm still here fighting.

Following a leg amputation to remove MRSA-infected tissue, a dressing is applied using the vacuum assisted closure technique to prevent further infection. (© **Dr. P. Marazzi/Photo Researchers, Inc.**)

A Skin Boil Turns into Flesh-Eating Disease

Andrew Chant

In the following selection, Andrew Chant of Queensland, Australia, recounts his experience of surviving necrotizing fasciitis (NF)—also known as "flesh-eating disease"—which can be triggered by infection with MRSA, *Streptococcus pyogenes*, or other virulent bacteria. Chant, a diabetic, noticed that an ingrown hair follicle on his leg had become a skin boil. His pain increased even after antibiotic treatment, and he was admitted to the hospital, where a specialist eventually recognized that he had developed gas gangrene stemming from NF. Chant underwent several surgeries to remove infected tissue, and at one point was given only a slim chance of surviving. He shares his story to reassure readers that it is possible to survive such a serious infection with only minimal damage.

My name is Andrew Chant and I'm a survivor of necrotizing fasciitis. I'm 30 years old and live in Queensland, Australia. I've now been home from hospital a month and wanted to share my story with you all in the hope that someone finds comfort and understanding from reading about my experience. I must say that I have benefited greatly from reading the stories of others . . . while recovering from this insidious disease.

My problems began in March 2010 when I had an ingrown hair follicle in the crease of my right leg. I am a Type II Diabetic and at that time had fairly poor diabetic control. The hair follicle gave me a little discomfort but nothing significant. I began feeling unwell around Sunday the 7th and by Wednesday the 10th of March the hair follicle had developed into a boil. Not wasting anytime I immediately made an appointment to see my Doctor who promptly inspected the boil, declared it infected and prescribed me antibiotics. Over the next two days the boil grew steadily more painful and finally burst on the evening of Friday the 12th. My Doctor had expected that this may occur so I wasn't unduly worried. By Sunday the 14th, however, the pain had increased to where I couldn't sit down for more than a few minutes at a time. I became increasingly more disoriented, was running a high temperature and was extremely thirsty. After some encouragement from my wife and mother, [I] decided to make an appointment with the After-Hours Clinic at my local Private Hospital.

An Intensifying Infection

After waiting about an hour in the waiting room I simply couldn't take the pain of sitting on the area any longer and asked if I could lie [down] while I waited to be seen by the doctor working in the clinic. Another 30 minutes or so later I was seen by the doctor and admitted to hospital. The Private Hospital was a good but small hospital with limited staff and resources. I felt sure though they'd get to the bottom of what was going on. I really have no memory of the Monday or Tuesday following my admittance.

My wife and parents told me that I experienced a lot of pain and that my Blood Glucose levels were very high. I remember waking up on the afternoon of Wednesday the 17th and feeling extremely sick. I was hyperventilating from severe acidosis and was extremely distressed. I was told that they were still waiting on test results that had been performed over the previous two days. Early in the afternoon however a nurse made a shocking discovery. There was now a hole in the crease of my other leg. When a finger was placed over the new hole gas was expelled out of the original site. A specialist was immediately called. He recognized immediately that I had gas gangrene stemming from necrotizing fasciitis. My scrotum had swelled to the size of a grapefruit and now all visitors had to be gowned and masked. The nearby General Hospital is a University Hospital and it was decided immediately that I be transferred there for urgent debridement surgery. After finding a surgeon at the General Hospital an ambulance was called to transfer me the five minutes between hospitals. The ambulance arrived two and a half hours later after a communication mix-up caused them to refuse to transport me. I arrived at the General Hospital in the evening of Wednesday the 17th and was immediately prepped for [the operating] theatre. This would be the last time I'd be conscious for a week.

> **FAST FACT**
>
> Debridement is the removal of dead, infected, or damaged tissue to improve the healing potential of the remaining healthy tissue.

Debridement and Intensive Care

In those two weeks I was worked on by an extremely skilled team of surgeons and nurses in the Intensive Care Unit [ICU]. All together I had around 8 debridement surgeries. There was a large open wound on the side of my leg where the boil had presented itself. It stretched for almost the entire crease. I also had a large section of tissue taken from the crease of my other leg. I also had about a third of

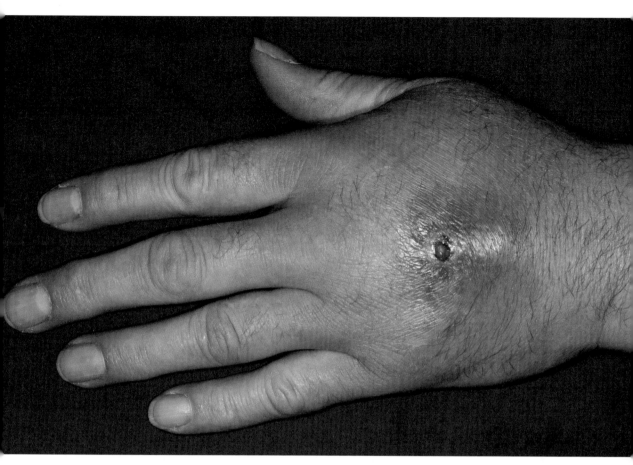

A MRSA infection can seem insignificant initially, but it soon develops into an abscess (shown), sometimes becoming gangrenous, as in the author's case.
(© Scott Camazine/Photo Researchers, Inc.)

my scrotum removed. I experienced no major organ failure during this time and began responding well to my IV antibiotics. I was briefly brought out of sedation at one point; however, my blood pressure began to drop and I became highly distressed so I was given another few days of sedation. I began to come around on Wednesday the [24th]. I can only remember images and voices from the previous week. I had tubes coming from just about every part of my body—a triple lumen CVC [central venous catheter] an arterial line for blood gas testing, a rectal tube to keep the wounds clean, a feeding tube, a catheter and the now famous Vac Dressing. Towards the end of my stay in ICU I had another couple of surgeries to begin closing my wounds. I became stronger over the next few days as I came to grips with what had occurred.

On Friday the [26th] I was able to stand for a few seconds and it was decided that I be moved to the Surgical Ward. It was here that I would have another three surgeries to change dressings and close up my still open wounds. The second of these would be a skin graft which proved to be very successful. Over the next few weeks I worked hard to regain my strength. My wounds also were healing well and by the time I was discharged on April 15 I was left with only two small(ish) open wounds. My wife continues to dress them—I am told they look better every day. At one stage I was only given a 25% chance of making it through but all of my major organs did me proud and didn't fail. I lost a fair amount of tissue and will have significant scarring. My scrotum had to be stretched and remodeled. I feel very lucky, however, to escape with everything important intact. Without the support of my wife and family I fear I might not have been so lucky. All of the staff that worked on me were fantastic and they should be extremely satisfied with the work they did and the outcome that they achieved. To all of you out there who are recovering or who are fighting this awful disease, I want you to know that there is light at the end of the tunnel. Contracting NF is not always fatal & it is possible to survive with minimal damage.

A Woman Recounts Her Husband's MRSA Scare

Christina Jones

Christina Jones maintains the blog *Marshall Jones' MRSA Story* at www.mrstory.com. In the following piece, Jones shares a personal anecdote that illustrates both the fear and the confusion accompanying a MRSA infection, for those infected and for those close to them. Christina Jones's husband, Marshall, was hospitalized and diagnosed with MRSA months after discovering his infection, which was initially diagnosed as a spider bite. Even though Marshall did survive, Jones's story illustrates what a difficult ordeal MRSA can be for patients and their loved ones.

My husband, Marshall Jones, was hospitalized on October 13, 2004 with an MRSA blood infection and was released 33 days later. Marshall's infection began at the end of August, 2004, when after a haircut and

SOURCE: Christina Jones, *Marshall Jones' MRSA Story: His Battle with a Community Acquired MRSA (CA-MRSA) Infection and Septicemia*, (blog), www.mrsastory.com, April 18, 2005. Copyright © 2005 by Christina Jones. All rights reserved. Reproduced by permission.

a neck shave (at home), he got an ingrown hair on the back of his neck. I plucked the hair out with tweezers on about day 2, but the wound just kept growing. It was about the size of a quarter and was a very nasty looking wound when he went to the doctor, about 4 days later.

The doctor took a culture of it, drained it, and sent him home with Bactrim (an antibiotic used for skin infections) and a diagnosis of a spider bite. After about another week or so, he went back to the doctor because the wound was just not healing. Dr. Daftarian opened it up deeper this time because she said there were pockets of infection underneath where she had drained it the first time. She gave him instructions (for me—since obviously he would need help with a wound on the back of his neck!) on how to pack the wound so it would keep draining, and gave him Levaquin antibiotic. The wound finally healed after we nursed it daily for a week or two. It healed up beautifully, and other than a pretty good scar, we thought we were finished with it. Boy were we wrong!

Day 1, Tuesday

Somewhere around midnight, Marshall began vomiting. At this point, I started looking on the internet for his problem, because we have (finally) ruled out normal back pain. And I have finally been convinced that he really does have a problem. He has big lumps of bunched up muscles at the small of his back, on both sides of his spine. I can be so hard headed sometimes. Ugh.

The best I could come up with was kidney stones, and we thought it was a pretty good diagnosis. I asked Marshall if he wanted to go to the Emergency Room, but he didn't want to yet. He didn't want to get the children up in the middle of the night if he didn't have to, because they had school (they are 7 and 10). I fell back asleep around 2 am, he was still up, sick as a dog. He hasn't had a decent bit of sleep since Saturday night.

About 5 am, Marshall woke me up and told me to call an ambulance, that he didn't want me to have to get the kids up, but I got right up, got the kids, and we were on the road in no time. I am sure it was just as fast as waiting on an ambulance would have been. As if I am going to stay here with sleeping kids while my husband goes into the ER!

When we got into the ER, Marshall told the man at the desk that he thought his kidneys were shutting down, and they got him right into triage, without the normal several hour wait in the ER waiting room. In triage, they asked him questions, weighed him (235lbs), showed him this ridiculous pain scale with smiley faces to try to get him to tell them how much pain he was in, took some blood, and his temperature. His temp was 104. They put him in a room in the ER, and pretty quickly came in with some insulin, as his blood sugar was 311, and they said he was diabetic. This was a first for us. Marshall had been told before that his sugar was a little on the high side, but never had he been told he had diabetes. Looking back, we should have known. His mothers side of the family is full of diabetes, and he has had alot of symptoms during the last year. Dr. Daftarian was consulted, and Marshall was given some Vicodin for his pain, but not too much, as they did not want to mask his pain until they knew what the problem was. Dr. Daftarian ordered an Xray and a CAT scan, which was done in the next couple of hours. I took the kids over to my father-in-law's house, and he took them to school for me.

After several hours, Dr. Daftarian admitted him to the hospital, room 243, in the general medical unit. Dr. D came in around noon to see Marshall. We told her about our thinking that it was a kidney stone. We asked about appendicitis, and because Marshall's infection on his neck was the first time we had seen Dr. Daftarian, we reminded her of that, and told her that it had healed up beautifully. Marshall was still nauseous, we wondered if that could be a Vicodin reaction. Dr. Daftarian started Marshall on IV antibiotics at this point, and again, I failed to note which one it was (for the last time!).

Day 2, Wednesday

Dr. Daftarian came in this morning, early, and reported that nothing significant was seen in the Xray or the CAT scan. She had both tests repeated. At this point, the staph infection in his neck from August was bugging me, and I was really starting to worry about it. When we had seen Dr. Daftarian the third time (in September, to check on his neck after we had been packing it), she told me that the infection was *Staphylococcus aureus*, but was NOT the antibiotic resistant variety (MRSA). I may have misunderstood her, but I remember that that was what I had heard her say, because I remember saying that was a relief that it was not MRSA. Regardless, I was still worried, because Staph in any form is dangerous. She said that his blood work results would be in soon, and then we would find out more.

> **FAST FACT**
>
> Most species of *Staphylococcus* bacteria are harmless to humans.

Dr. D came back in a little later, probably around noon, and said that a kidney stone could have possibly been missed by the Xray and CAT scan, and ordered a sonogram, which would tell us something for sure. She said that Marshall was looking a little better to her this afternoon. After she left, they did the sonogram, which showed no stone. She told us she was calling in an infectious disease specialist.

I had to go get the children from the bus, but on my way out, I told Marshall's nurse, Dee, that I thought Marshall looked worse, not better—his breathing was very rapid and shallow.

While I was gone, Dr. Lemos had been there. He had the results of the blood work, and indeed it was *Staphylococcus aureus*, and MRSA to make things worse. When Marshall heard that, his heart rate shot up to 225 beats per minute (bpm), and they put him into the ICU immediately and started him on vancomycin. In the ICU, there are strict visitation hours, but when the nurse (Dee) called me to let me know they were putting him in there, she said I could come find her, and she would take me on into the ICU when I got there.

So, when I got back to the hospital, a cardiologist, Dr. Schwartz, had been consulted, and ordered an ECG. They were looking for the source of infection, and thought they might find it on the heart valve, which is apparently a common place for *S. aureus* to set up shop. Marshall's heart beat was too fast however, for a good evaluation, so Dr. Schwartz said they would repeat it tomorrow.

They are giving Marshall good drugs now (morphine) but he still can't sleep. I talked to TaShondra, Marshall's ICU nurse, about the possibility of a ventilator, because I really thought his rapid breathing was what was causing him to stay awake. She said she was just getting ready to mention this to me, and that it would be likely that that would be what happened.

Dr. Lemos (infectious disease) thinks that there must be an abscess in Marshall's lower back (due to the pain there). He ordered an MRI, but the machine is not working today (and they said Marshall is too unstable right now anyway–likely story!), but they will get one just as soon as they can.

I cannot remember what I did with the children on this day, but I know I slept at home, and I think they did too.

Day 8, Tuesday

I talked to Dr. Lemos this morning. The doctors are so hard to catch in the ICU. I am sure they avoid visiting during visitation hours! I had a big list of questions.

I have made a list of questions for Dr. Lemos:

We need time to talk, do we need to make an appointment with you?

Do we need to be gloved and masked when we are in here?

Relatives think we need to move him to Methodist . . . any thoughts?

Our animals at home, could they have caused this? (Petunia)

Do the kids and I need to be treated for staph?

Where did this come from?

What are you looking for to know he is improving, and how fast should he beginning to improve?

Dr. Lemos said that the Staph in his neck and then in his blood was not caused by his ingrown hair. Diabetes made his immune system compromised, and the ingrown hair infection just went out of control. I told him what Dr. Daftarian had told us in August about using the Hibiclens soap, Bactroban, and Lysol, and he said that was fine, that the rest of us shouldn't have to worry about getting this infection. All we needed to do was to be aware of wounds, and appropriately cleanse and treat them. He said that Staph is on everyone's skin all of the time, and normally our bodies can deal with that bacteria if it gets into a cut, but sometimes, because of a compromised immune system, it can manage to take over. Dr. Lemos also said that it might take a while, but Marshall was going to be ok!

I also saw Dr. Spencer today, he said that the ventilator would come off in 3–5 days, when they get much more fluid off of him, and that he would probably be on antibiotics for another 6 weeks.

2 Weeks Out of the Hospital

We have passed the 2 week mark now. Marshall had a ROUGH day today, he has been very very lightheaded today, and a little bit over the weekend. His blood pressure this morning was 138/100 and his temperature was 94.6, and I took it several times. Very weird. He took a hot shower and drank some coffee. We went to see Dr. Daftarian after lunch, and everything was pretty much back to normal. He has gained a few pounds, and is up to 200.

It is our anniversary today, and would you believe he managed to send me flowers? He is so thoughtful, and precious to me, I am so thankful he is still with me.

GLOSSARY

abscess An accumulation of white, yellow, or greenish matter known as pus surrounded by reddened tissue. Staph bacteria are the most common cause of abscesses.

antibiotic resistance A form of drug resistance in which a microorganism develops the ability to survive exposure to the antibiotics intended to kill it.

antibiotics Also known as antibacterials, these are drugs used to treat infections caused by bacteria.

bacteriophage A virus that infects and destroys bacteria.

CA-MRSA Community-acquired MRSA.

colonization The process of occupation and increase in number of microorganisms at a specific site.

epidemiologist A scientist who studies the transmission and control of diseases.

HA-MRSA Hospital-acquired MRSA.

methicillin An antibiotic developed in 1959 to treat penicillin-resistant bacterial infections. It has been replaced by more stable antibiotics and is no longer manufactured.

MRSA Methicillin-resistant *Staphylococcus aureus*. Even though methicillin is no longer in use as a medicine, MRSA (pronounced "mersa") is still the term usually used to describe *Staphylococcus aureus* strains that are resistant to penicillins.

necrotizing fasciitis A relatively rare infection of the deeper layers of the skin and subcutaneous tissues. Most often caused by Group A *Streptococcus* bacteria, it can also be caused by MRSA. Also known as flesh-eating disease.

pathogen	A disease-causing agent, such as a bacterium, virus, or fungus.
penicillin	A group of antibiotics developed from the *Penicillium* fungus.
resistance	Immunity developed within a species (especially bacteria) to an antibiotic or other drug. In bacteria, genetic mutations can render them invulnerable to the action of antibiotics.
selection pressure	Factors that influence the evolution of an organism. Human overuse of antibiotics provides a selection pressure for the development of antibiotic resistance in bacteria.
septicemia	Bacterial infection of the bloodstream from an originally infected site.
strain	A genetic variant or subtype of a bacterium or other microorganism.
Staphylococcus	The genus of at least forty species of bacteria, most of which are harmless and reside on the skin and mucous membranes of humans and other organisms.
Staphylococcus aureus	The bacterium responsible for the majority of staph infections, which most often infect the skin and mucous membranes.
superbug	Informal term for an antibiotic-resistant bacterium.
vancomycin	An antibiotic, usually reserved as a "drug of last resort," to be used only when other antibiotics have failed.
virulence	The relative ability of a disease organism to overcome the body's defenses. A highly virulent organism is one that can readily overcome the immune system.
VRSA	(Pronounced "versa") Vancomycin-resistant *Staphylococcus aureus.*

CHRONOLOGY

Late 1880s	Scottish surgeon Alexander Ogston identifies the *Staphylococcus aureus* bacterium.
1928	British scientist Alexander Fleming discovers the first antibiotic, penicillin.
1941	Penicillin becomes available in England and the United States. The first penicillin-resistant *S. aureus* is reported a short time later.
Late 1940s	Twenty-five percent of *S. aureus* bacteria in hospitals are penicillin-resistant.
1958	Vancomycin, currently considered an antibiotic of last resort, is introduced.
1959	Methicillin, a beta-lactamase-resistant penicillin, is licensed in England.
1960	English bacteriologist Patricia Jevons discovers methicillin-resistant *S. aureus* (MRSA) while testing bacterial samples for a study.
1961	Doctors encounter the first MRSA infections.
1961–1967	Several outbreaks of MRSA occur in Western European and Australian hospitals.
1968	The first US hospital outbreak of MRSA occurs at Boston City Hospital in Massachusetts.
1974	MRSA accounts for 2 percent of hospital staph infections in the United States.
1982	A large outbreak of MRSA occurs among intravenous drug users in Detroit, Michigan.

Mid-1990s	There are scattered reports of community-acquired MRSA (CA-MRSA) infections in US children.
1997	Hospital-acquired MRSA (HA-MRSA) accounts for 50 percent of hospital staph infections.
1998	University of Chicago researchers report a twenty-five-fold increase in CA-MRSA from 1993 to1995.
1999	The Centers for Disease Control and Prevention reports the deaths of four otherwise healthy children from CA-MRSA.
2001	USA300 becomes the predominant strain of CA-MRSA in the United States.
2002	Doctors first identify vancomycin-resistant *S. aureus* (VRSA) in Michigan and Pennsylvania.
2002	The University of Chicago finds that new cases of CA-MRSA are genetically distinct from hospital strains.
2005	Athletes, military recruits, the incarcerated, emergency room patients, HIV patients, urban children, men who have sex with men, and indigenous populations are identified as being at high risk for CA-MRSA.
2008	University of Iowa researchers discover MRSA in more than 70 percent of pigs they tested on farms in Iowa and Illinois.
2009	CA-MRSA infections are common in most US cities; CA-MRSA infection and asymptomatic colonization are less common outside of the United States.
2011	Over 95 percent of *S. aureus* worldwide is penicillin-resistant and 60 percent is methicillin-resistant.

ORGANIZATIONS TO CONTACT

The editors have compiled the following list of organizations concerned with the issues debated in this book. The descriptions are derived from materials provided by the organizations. All have publications or information available for interested readers. The list was compiled on the date of publication of the present volume; the information provided here may change. Be aware that many organizations take several weeks or longer to respond to inquiries, so allow as much time as possible.

American Council on Science and Health (ACSH)
1995 Broadway, 2nd Fl., New York, NY 10023-5860
(212) 362-7704
fax: (212) 362-4919
e-mail: acsh@acsh.org
website: www.acsh.org

The ACSH is a consumer education consortium concerned with, among other topics, issues related to health and disease. The council maintains the website HealthFactsandFears.com, which provides informational articles and health updates such as "FDA Antibiotic Regulations Under the Microscope," and "Incentives Mulled for Drug Makers to Target 'Superbugs.'" The ACSH homepage includes links to recent articles, editorials, and speeches on diseases, food safety, and pharmaceuticals.

Centers for Disease Control and Prevention (CDC)
1600 Clifton Rd.
Atlanta, GA 30333
(800) 232-4636 or
(888) 232-6348
website: www.cdc.gov

A branch of the US Department of Health and Human Services, the CDC serves as the national focus for developing and applying disease prevention and control, environmental health, and health promotion and health education activities designed to improve the health of people in the United States. An A–Z index, fact sheets on MRSA, and links to resources and articles such as "Personal Prevention of MRSA Skin Infections" are all available on its website.

Food Safety Consortium (FSC)
110 Agriculture Bldg.
University of
Arkansas
Fayetteville, AR
72701
(479) 575-5647
fax: (479) 575-7531
e-mail: dedmark@
uark.edu
website: www.uark
.edu

Congress established the FSC, consisting of researchers from the University of Arkansas, Iowa State University, and Kansas State University, in 1988 through a special Cooperative State Research Service Grant. The FSC conducts extensive investigation into all areas of poultry, beef, and pork production. The consortium publishes *Meat and Poultry,* a journal for meat and poultry processors, with links to articles such as "No Evidence That Eating, Handling MRSA-Tainted Food Ups Human Risk."

Infectious Diseases Society of America (IDSA)
1300 Wilson Blvd.
Ste. 300, Arlington
VA 22209
website: www.id
society.org

The IDSA is a group representing physicians, scientists, and other health care professionals who specialize in infectious diseases. Its purpose is to improve the health of individuals, communities, and society by promoting excellence in patient care, education, research, public health, and prevention as it relates to infectious diseases. The society publishes two scholarly journals, *The Journal of Infectious Diseases* and *Clinical Infectious Diseases.* IDSA's online index includes information on antimicrobial resistance and links to articles such as "Clinical Practice Guidelines by the Infectious Diseases Society of America for the Treatment of Methicillin-Resistant *Staphylococcus* Infections in Adults and Children."

MRSA Survivors Network (MSN)
PO Box 241, Hinsdale, IL 60522
(630) 325-4354
e-mail: info@mrsa
survivors.org
website: www.mrsa
survivors. org

Founded in 2003, the MSN was the first nonprofit consumer organization in the United States to raise the alarm about the MRSA epidemic and other multidrug-resistant, health-care–acquired infections. MSN partners with health care professionals, health care companies, and consumer advocates in its mission to stop MRSA-related infections and deaths. Its website provides information about community-acquired MRSA, MRSA in pets, MRSA in athletes, and related topics, as well as a link to stories written by MRSA survivors.

National Foundation for Infectious Diseases (NFID)
4733 Bethesda Ave.
Ste. 750, Bethesda
MD 20814
(301) 656-0003
fax: (301) 907-0878
e-mail: info@nfid.org
website: www.nfid
.org

This foundation is a nonprofit philanthropic organization that supports disease research through grants and fellowships and educates the public about research, treatment, and prevention of infectious diseases. The NFD publishes a newsletter, *Double Helix,* and its website features a "Continuing Medical Education" (CME) page that links to the MRSA CME Learning Center and a fact sheet on community-associated MRSA.

National Institute of Allergy and Infectious Diseases (NIAID)
Office of Communications and Government Relations
6610 Rockledge Dr.
MSC 6612, Bethesda
MD 20892-6612
(301) 402-1663
fax: (301) 402-0120
website: www.niaid
.nih.gov

The NIAID conducts and supports research to better understand, treat, and ultimately prevent infectious, immunologic, and allergic diseases. Infections and antimicrobial resistance constitute two of the NIAID's areas of research, and many resources and articles are available from the NIAID on these topics, including "Combating Drug Resistance with Basic Research" and "New Approach to Fighting Staph Infections." The website includes a searchable database with links to fact sheets and updates on MRSA.

National Necrotizing Fasciitis Foundation (NNFF)
ATTN: Donna Batdorff
2730 Porter St. SW
Grand Rapids, MI
49509
e-mail: www.nnff.org
website: nnfffeb@
aol.com

The mission of the NNFF is to raise public awareness about necrotizing fasciitis (also known as flesh-eating disease), specifically regarding symptom recognition and preventative measures. The NNFF also promotes research, provides educational resources, and offers support to those affected by necrotizing fasciitis. Its website includes links to fact sheets, journal articles, discussion groups, and survivors' stories.

US Food and Drug Administration (FDA)
10903 New Hampshire Ave., Silver Spring, MD 20993
(888) 463-6332
website: www.fda.gov

The FDA's mission is to promote and protect the public health by helping safe and effective foods, drugs, and medicines reach the market in a timely manner, and to monitor such products for continued safety after they are in use. The FDA publishes the magazine *FDA Consumer* as well as various government documents, reports, fact sheets, and press announcements. The index available at its website provides links to brochures on the judicious use of antimicrobials in farm animals.

FOR FURTHER READING

Books

Hernan R. Chang, *MRSA and Staphylococcal Infections*, 2nd ed. Jacksonville, FL: Hernan R. Chang, 2008.

Karl S. Drlica and David S. Perlin, *Antibiotic Resistance: Understanding and Responding to an Emerging Crisis.* Upper Saddle River, NJ: FT Press, 2011.

Thomas Hausler, *Viruses vs. Superbugs: A Solution to the Antibiotics Crisis?* New York: Macmillan, 2007.

Maryn McKenna, *Beating Back the Devil.* New York: Free Press, 2008.

Maryn McKenna, *Superbug: The Fatal Menace of MRSA.* New York: Free Press, 2010.

Joseph Parazoo, *Surviving MRSA: Learn How to Protect Yourself.* Seattle: CreateSpace, 2009.

L.A. Reynolds and E.M. Tansey, eds., *Superbugs and Superdrugs: A History of MRSA.* London: Wellcome Trust Centre for the History of Medicine at UCL, 2008.

Jessica Snyder Sachs, *Good Germs, Bad Germs: Health and Survival in a Bacterial World.* New York: Hill and Wang, 2008.

Michael A. Schmidt, *Beyond Antibiotics: Strategies for Living in a World of Emerging Infections and Antibiotic-Resistant Bacteria*, 3rd ed. Berkeley, CA: North Atlantic Books, 2009.

Brad Spellberg, *Rising Plague: The Global Threat from Deadly Bacteria and Our Dwindling Arsenal to Fight Them.* Amherst, NY: Prometheus Books, 2009.

Thomasine E. Lewis Tilden, *Help! What's Eating My Flesh? Runaway Staph and Strep Infections!* New York: Franklin Watts, 2008.

Periodicals and Internet Sources

Michael J. Berens and Ken Armstrong, "How Our Hospitals Unleashed a MRSA Epidemic," *Seattle Times*, November 16, 2008.

Michael Booi, "Sidelined by . . . Infection? Evaluating, Managing, and Preventing MRSA," *Coach and Athletic Director*, February 2010.

David Briggs, "The Most-Feared Opponent: MRSA Worries Coaches, Trainers," *Columbia (MO) Daily Tribune*, August 6, 2009.

H. Cook et al. "Heterosexual Transmission of Community-Associated Methicillin-Resistant *Staphylococcus Aureus*," *Clinical and Infectious Diseases*, vol. 44, 2007.

Karen Dente, "Antibacterial Properties Could Make Nectar an Effective Treatment for Sores that Refuse to Mend," *Los Angeles Times*, September 10, 2007.

Economist, "Fighting Superbugs: Drug-Resistant Infections," June 13, 2009.

Farmers Guardian, "New Strain of MRSA Places Farms Under the Microscope," June 10, 2011.

Emily A. Kane, "Fighting Infections: Learn How Essential Oils Can Help Resolve Antibiotic-Resistant Skin Infections," *Better Nutrition*, June 2009.

Gina Kolata, "Scientists Unlock a Mystery of Staph," *New York Times*, December 16, 2010.

Nicholas D. Kristof, "Our Pigs, Our Food, Our Health," *New York Times*, March 12, 2009.

Lillian Kwon, "Gay Outcry Downplays MRSA," *Christian Post*, January 25, 2008. www.christianpost.com.

Mayo Clinic, "Staph Infections," www.mayoclinic.com/health/staph-infections/DS00973, June 9, 2011.

Meredith Melnick, "Thought Bedbugs Were Bad? Try Bedbugs with MRSA," *Time*, May 12, 2011.

Christian Nordqvist, "Bed Bugs Carrying MRSA and VER Superbugs," *Medical News Today*, May 14, 2011.

PR Newswire, "New in Vitro Study Data Show That Wound Dressing with Silver Kills MRSA and Other Superbugs' Resistant to Antibiotics," April 15, 2011.

Lisa Priest, "Superbug MRSA Spreading Fast, Report Warns," *Globe and Mail* (Toronto), March 27, 2008.

Sabin Russell, "Drug-Resistant Staph, Once Confined to Hospitals, Spreads from Cities with Large Gay Populations," *San Francisco Chronicle*, January 15, 2008.

States News Service, "Science: New Method for Tracing MRSA's Spread May Improve Infection Control," January 21, 2010.

Lena H. Sun, "Bedbugs May Play Role in Spread of Drug-Resistant Bacteria MRSA, Study Finds," *Washington Post*, May 11, 2011.

Mark Trumbull, "Staph in Meat: Are U.S. Cattle and Poultry Over-Drugged?," *Christian Science Monitor*, April 16, 2011.

Stephanie Woodard, "The Superbug in Your Supermarket," *Prevention*, August 2009.

INDEX

A

Abscess, *15, 40,* 40–41, *101*

Acanthamoeba, 23

AIDS, deaths from MRSA *vs., 69*

Annals of American Medicine (journal), 68

Antibacterial agents, numbers approved in US, *91*

Antibiotic resistance, 12–13, 25
cause of, 18, 27
linked to antibiotic use in livestock, 29, 44, 47–51

Antibiotic-resistant infections, rise of, 24–29

Antibiotics
increase risk for developing resistant infections, 28
overuse on factory farms allowed MRSA to enter food supply, 43–52
use in livestock, 29
Antibodies, workings of, *39*

Association for Professionals in Infection Control and Epidemiology (APIC), 86

Austin, Jeff, 81

Autor, Deborah, 90, 91

B

Bacteriophages, 13, 16, 21

Barrett, Tom, 75

Bedbugs, *61*
bites from, *65*
increase in infestations of, 62
life cycle of, *67*
percentage of adults reporting, by neighborhood poverty level, *63*
scientists need to investigate potential MRSA threat from, 59–63
transmission of MRSA by, has not been proven, 64–67

Bennett, Michael, 88

Bouchard, Lucien, 44

Brown, Sherrod, 59, 60–63

C

CA-MRSA. *See* Community-associated MRSA

Canadian Integrated Program for Antimicrobial Resistance Surveillance (CIPARS), 50

Canadian Medical Association Journal, 51

CDC. *See* Centers for Disease Control and Prevention

Ceftiofur, 50, 51

Centers for Disease Control and Prevention (CDC), 11, 25, 66, 75